Postcards from Paradise

Romancing Key West

June Keith

Palm Island Press
Key West, Florida

Postcards From Paradise
Romancing Key West
by June Keith

Published by
PALM ISLAND PRESS
411 Truman Avenue, Key West, Florida 33040 U.S.A.
pipress@earthlink.net
SAN 298-4024

LIBRARY OF CONGRESS CATALOGING-IN-PUBLICATION DATA

Keith, June
    Postcards from Paradise : Romancing Key West/ June Keith
    p. cm.
    Includes index
    ISBN-13: 978-0-9743524-1-1
    ISBN-10: 0-9743524-1-1

    1. Key West (Fla.)—Social life and customs. 2. Key West (Fla.)—History. I.Title

F319.K4K45 2006   **2006931317**
917.59'41

Table of Contents

Tom Netting

Queen of all she sees. There is something wonderful in the air here, an earthy perfume of hot sun, salt water, sweat and sun tan lotion, that makes every day steamy and seductively romantic. Tom Netting took this photo of me on the roof of the La Concha Hotel on Duval Street. I'm giving Key West a great big hug. I love Key West!

Paradise Lost & Found

I spent my last summer on the mainland working as a go-go girl. The booking agent's office was on Broadway, right in the heart of New York City, and sometimes I felt like I really was in show biz, visiting his office and sitting around with the other dancers waiting for our directives to the go-go bars of Reading, Pa., or Marlboro, Mass. It was an interesting way to see America. A red-headed girl named Sabrina and I danced our way from state to state, eating in diners and visiting tattoo parlors. (Neither of us actually got a tattoo, but we considered it very seriously and very often.) After a week or two in one place, we'd move on to the next. Sabrina drove while I read Dorothy Parker stories aloud. Sabrina wanted an education. I wanted to write. In our separate ways, we believed ourselves to be on the road to our personal goals. And we were.

When winter loomed I began to grow restless. I didn't want to spend the winter in gloomy Manhattan. I had waited out a previous winter on a sailboat in Key West. I had made my liv-

ing dancing afternoons at the Esquire Lounge. Evenings I sat
on the bow of the boat writing poetry by the light of the
moon. But life in Key West that first winter seemed too slow
and too lazy. I missed New England angst. When spring came
I headed north.

Six months later, I couldn't wait to get back to the island.

"New York is the center of the universe, baby!" the booking
agent said when I told him that I was heading back to Key
West. "You wanna write? You gotta stay right here. New York is
where all the great writers live!"

Sabrina rented a sixth-floor walk up in Soho. Eventually
she married a college professor and earned a couple of
degrees.

I drove to Key West. Alone. The trip took two days. Upon
arriving, I was at the intersection of White Street and Truman
Avenue when a guy whose name I never knew recognized me
from the previous winter, climbed up onto the hood of my car
like a monkey, and pressed his lips against the windshield with
a big kiss. "Hi!" he said. Then he jumped off, waved and went
on his way.

I was smitten then and I still am today - not with the guy;
that was the last time I ever saw him - but with his spontaneity.
It was an analogy for the spirit of the island. I knew in that
moment that I had made the right decision. I'd found my
home.

That was 18 years ago. Since then I've been a wife (twice)
and mother, radio sales person, news reporter, administrative
assistant to the mayor, political campaign manager, hospital
public relations director, art gallery saleswoman, tour guide,
bartender, waitress and free-lance writer.

I have finally learned to accept the fact that desk jobs don't
suit my metabolism. I need action, and I get it five nights a
week at the Lighthouse Cafe, where I work as a waitress.

I meet and chat with at least 100 new people a week. I ask

them where they're from and what they do. They ask me, "How long have you been here?"

"I've lived here in paradise for 19 wonderful years," I answer. Then I watch their faces turn soft and dreamy. They want to live here, too. They are lost. I am found.

"So you like it then?" they ask helplessly.

"Wouldn't dream of living anywhere else," I say. And I mean it.

Key West is my greatest love affair. At first, the attachment was powerful and bewildering and I resented its hold on me. But as I've grown and changed my love has mellowed. I am no longer captive; I choose Key West. I have roots and a history here. I have family here and friends I love like family. I know hundreds of people simply through seeing them and exchanging hellos in the grocery store or at the bank. I don't know their names or what they do. All I know is that they live in Key West, too.

After 19 years, there are no strangers in paradise.

Sandy Arena

*Halloween, 1974. Ft. Lauderdale. I made pasties with Elmer's Glue
and a jar of red glitter. I called myself a go-go girl and won a costume
contest at the Playpen Bar. I loved being a go-go girl, a career path
I was later to follow in earnest. But peeling the Elmer's glue off my
nipples was a terrible ordeal. At the Esquire Lounge we weren't
required to wear pasties, thank goodness.*

Glitz, Glitter & Grind

Last night the Esquire Lounge closed its doors for good, ending a glorious quarter century as Key West's premiere palace of glitz, glitter and grind.

In the 25 years since the go-go bar began featuring topless dancers, owner Buddy Brewer estimates that over 7,000 girls have performed on the Esquire's tiny stage. Some of them still live in Key West. Others phone in from time to time. And at Christmas, Buddy receives greetings from all over.

"I'll get a card from somebody named Sarah Smith, and I'll wonder 'Now who the hell is that?' " Buddy laughs.

"Then I'll remember - oh! That's Star! The dancer. Because when girls dance, they give themselves stage names like 'Star' or 'Flame' or 'Jewel.' "

"When I danced I called myself Goldie," I said to him.
"Oh, yeah," Buddy grinned. "We've had a couple dozen Goldies."

When I arrived in Key West in 1974, dancing at the Esquire Lounge was one of the few jobs available to adventurous young ladies like my traveling companion Cammie Lee and me.

Cammie had arranged for us to spend a week in the Eaton Street apartment of the friend of a friend. Within hours of our arrival in Key West, however, we decided we wanted to settle permanently on this magnificent sunny isle - or at least for the winter. But how? The money we'd earned waiting tables during the previous summer in New York was dwindling fast.

Every morning we dined at Shorty's on Duval Street and pondered our futures. Over coffee and cigarettes we perused the help-wanted ads in the newspapers that other diners left behind. The list of jobs was pitifully brief.

One ad appeared daily. It promised $10.50 an hour to attractive girls willing to dance topless at the Esquire Lounge. Cammie and I giggled over the ad for a few days, but as time went on, $10.50 an hour began to sound very appealing.

"Let's just go see what it's like," I suggested.

"But we're not qualified," Cammie reminded me, waving her hand across her washboard-flat chest while glaring at my own bony top.

Eventually I convinced Cammie to check out topless dancing, a job I figured couldn't be any more humiliating than waiting on tables in a French maid costume at a Holiday Inn which is what I'd done up north. So we drove to Searstown, found the Esquire, and asked for Buddy, who quickly appeared to conduct our interviews and auditions.

Since I was the more daring one, I jumped up on stage first. I danced my very best, kicking, twirling and smiling brightly at Buddy who seemed to barely look at me. Meanwhile, a couple of guys playing pool put down their cue sticks and began to stare at me. I loved their stares and Goldie the Go-Go Girl was born.

Buddy explained that dancers received $3.50 for a 20-minute set, and they danced one set per hour. It took 3 hours

to accumulate that $10.50, but only one hour of actual danc-
ing. There were tips, too, he said.

"I've got to think about this for a while," Cammie stam-
mered. "Ah, I'll come back later for my audition. "

"Hey, don't worry about it. You're both hired," Buddy said.
"You start tomorrow."

"Gee, that's weird," I said, grabbing my clothes and trying
to catch up with Cammie who had bolted for the door and the
sunshine beyond the dark, dank interior of the Esquire
Lounge. "He doesn't even know if you can dance!"

Cammie found a job the next day at a health food store,
while I began my short career at the Esquire Lounge. Within
a few months I had a boyfriend who ordered me to quit my
go-go gig.

But that first evening at the Esquire Lounge I earned $32
in tips. The next morning, and for many mornings thereafter,
I picked up the breakfast tab at Shorty's.

Michael Lee

My first husband, Mike Perez, and me. He made me laugh.
He made me cry. Together we made a terrific child. And then we
parted. Who knows why we love who we love? I wish I could be
as sure of other things in my life as I am of my love for my
first husband. I will always love Mike Perez.

My First Ex

The first time I saw him, I knew he would be the father of my children. The first time he saw me, he says, he thought he was seeing an angel. One of our first dates was Thanksgiving dinner at his mother's house.

"My father will be there, and my stepfather, too," he explained as we drove to the celebration. "They're all friends, and they all celebrate together on holidays. Hey, they have kids together - how could we do it any other way?"

How indeed, I marveled, as I sat in the car next to the man with whom I was to share the next five years of my life. His descriptions of his family - and his life growing up in Key West, where natives are called "Conchs" - were better than any fiction I had ever read, better than any story I could have imagined.

A few days before Christmas, he gave me a tiny gold conch shell on a chain.

"I hope you'll always remember Key West," he said. "I hope you'll always remember your Conch."

On Christmas Day, we went to the dog track on Stock Island, and then had dinner with his family. The family seemed happy to see me, surprised and pleased to see him again with the same woman.

On New Year's Day, we sat in the living room of his ramshackle Conch house, sipping steaming cafe con leche from the M & M Laundromat and Coffee Shop, surveying the wreckage from the previous night's party.

"What a mess," I said.

"When are you going to clean it up?" he asked.

"Me?" I asked.

"You're my woman, aren't you?" he said softly, warming me through to the core with just his eyes. "Don't women take care of their men?"

Like a happy puppy, I sprung from the couch and set about my cleaning duties. A few days later, I moved in with my master.

We had a lot of fun in those early days. We visited his various friends and relatives, and on Saturday nights we danced Latin to the Buddy Chavez Combo.

Life was sweet, sexy and . . . confusing.

I quickly learned that according to his romantic code, women were to look lovely, keep house, cook and care for their men. Meanwhile, the men were free to roam, from sunup till sundown and sometimes all the way 'round to sunup again. Women were to report their activities to men, but men had no such obligations to women. It was considered bad form for a woman to question her man about his comings or goings. She was also forbidden to be jealous or possessive. Yet a man was jealous and possessive beyond all reason.

I learned a new form of misery, which was relieved, temporarily, by the dramas of my wedding, pregnancy, childbirth and new motherhood. Still, we couldn't make marriage work. I wanted him, but I wanted so much more, too. Giving me freedom to explore went against everything he had ever learned about men and women. He couldn't do it. I couldn't bear the unfairness of him being free when I was not.

The day our divorce became final we had dinner with friends. We laughed our heads off. We always laughed a lot. He's a very funny man. Then I went home, alone, and cried until I couldn't cry anymore.

I'm married to the man I'm supposed to be married to now. My ex has finally met the right person, too.

He was my first husband, and I was his first wife, but we have both changed enormously in the 15 years since our wedding day. Today we're friends. Friends with a long, gutsy history. Friends for life. It feels right.

I still wear my gold conch from time to time. And whenever I see the man who gave it to me, my heart jars a bit, and I think - there he is, the father of my child.

Rene Rojas collection

The El Dorado. Havana, Cuba. 1946. Grampa is the fourth guy from the left. The El Dorado had four orchestra pits, and in one, an all-girl band playing in turns. Grampa and his Key West friends spent many weekends in Cuba. Back then, round-trip airfare to Havana was $12.

Grampa's
Wild Blue Yonder

O ne of my extended family's favorite tales of old Key
West is the one about Grampa, my former father-in-
law, joining the Navy.

Mike Perez was born on Packer Street, and had never been
further from home than Stock Island when he enlisted in
1943. He was 16 years old, and absurdly naive, but smart
enough to alter the date on his identification and trick his way
into the service.

"I was looking for adventure," he shrugs, "I wanted to see
the world."

At boot camp in Jacksonville, Mike was served his first taste
of fresh vegetables, an experience he immediately described
in a letter home.

"Mama," he wrote, "today I had something yellow and wonderful to eat. It's called squash, and if you ever see it in the
store, you should try it. It's delicious!"

Until then, his Cuban-born mother had served her family

mostly beans and rice. The only vegetable he'd had was canned string beans, after which he'd been nicknamed.

"I was called 'Stringbean' or 'Jimmy Durante' because my nose was so big and the rest of me was skinny as a string bean."

The Navy changed all that. Mike loved the cuisine, and ate plenty whenever it was offered. Within a few months he'd gained 40 pounds.

"Everybody complained about the food!" Mike says. "But not me. I'd never had it so good."

Right after that first wonderful meal in boot camp, the new recruits were ordered to shower. Mike hesitated, certain that he'd somehow misunderstood the directive.

"What are you waiting for, Perez?" the chief officer asked him.

"I can't shower now," Mike balked. "I just finished eating!"

"Are you trying to make a fool of me?" the officer demanded, incredulously.

All of his young life Mike had been cautioned that certain death would follow were one to encounter water within 2 hours of eating. This applied to swimming and bathing, and even having a haircut. As a child he'd witnessed a man die of a heart attack in a barbershop chair, the result, his elders told him, of having a haircut too soon after a meal.

"So I took a shower, but I was certain it would be the last thing I ever did," Mike says. "I turned on the water, and I screamed as it hit my head. But I didn't die."

This he also reported in the letter to his mother.

The Navy enlightened him in other ways, too. He'd grow up poor, but this he did not know until he ventured into to world and began comparing growing-up stories with other sailors.

On several cross-country train transports Mike, who'd only known salt water, palm trees and summer weather, was astounded to see America's variety of topographies and climates.

He loved Oregon, and hated Maryland. When his ship anchored for a month in Baltimore, it snowed a lot and the temperature was so frigid he could not bear to go outdoors.

His ship eventually participated in the invasion of Okinawa, and Mike vividly recalls the relief and shipboard revelry when Japan surrendered in 1945, ending the war and sending his ship home.

Ultimately, he says, his great adventure taught him how much he did not know, and how much he would never know about the whole wide world.

"Now," he says, "I'm 71 years old and I don't know anything. If somebody asks my advice, I say 'You should have asked me when I was 16. Then, I knew everything.' "

*George (left) and Nestor clowning it up in Mexico City,
a few hours before the earthquake.*

Contributed by Nery Belors

Yellow Bird

For the past few months I've been meaning to go by and see my friend George Lee. He's been very ill. Last winter he was diagnosed with lung cancer.

"We could send you to Miami for chemotherapy," his doctor told him.

"Will it cure me?" George asked.

"Well, no," the doctor answered.

So George went back to the house he shared with his longtime companion, Nestor, their little dog and a yellow canary, and prepared to die.

George and I became friends 11 years ago. I was newly on my own then, having just left my marriage. I was scared, but determined to make my divorce work. On my first night in my new home, George, who lived next door, invited me over for a drink. As we chatted and laughed over drinks and cigarettes it soon became obvious that we two were in for some good times. We clicked real fast, and real hard. Finally, I stood up to say good night.

"We're going to have a lot of fun, June," George said, hugging me sweetly. "This is perfect. I'm gay, and you're gay, and..."

"I'm not gay, George," I interrupted.

"But I heard you were!" he said, suddenly releasing me from the hug. "Isn't that why you left your husband?"

George eventually accepted my heterosexuality and cocktail hour became a regular part of our evenings. Every night we sat on George's deck and discussed the day's events. Sometimes we chatted in the morning before work, as I stood in my bathroom combing my hair and George watered his plants or fed his bird. George kept several little birds in a large cage adjacent to my house. I would often hear him talking patiently to the happily chirping birds, trying to get them to talk back to him. They never did learn to speak. One morning George found them gone. A snake, with two egg-sized lumps in his middle, was trapped in the cage. He had gone in through a square in the wire mesh cage and swallowed George's birds. After his meal, he'd been too lumpy to escape through the same hole.

I watched from my bathroom window as George, with slow and methodic movements, gently released the snake from the cage. He watched it slither away and disappear beneath a bougainvillea bush. Then he sat down, lighted a cigarette, and stared at the empty cage. George missed those birds for a long time. He truly loved them, just as he loved all delicate and beautiful things.

A couple of years after my arrival, George met Nestor and our nightly sessions took on a new dimension. Nestor loved to cook. And we all loved to eat. We still talked late into the night. Nestor told us about his childhood in Cuba, and George talked about his in Key West.

I remarried. My new husband, Michael, enjoyed conversation with George and Nestor as much as I did, and we quick-

ly became a foursome. He shared my disappointment when
they moved. Although their new house was only seven blocks
away, our visits with George and Nestor became rare.
Occasionally we phoned them, or bumped into Nestor at the
grocery store. By the time we heard of George's illness, it had
been several years since we four had dined together.

"We've got to visit George," I said to Michael every few
weeks.

Michael agreed. But we never did see George again and
early Tuesday morning he died. George's passing had been
peaceful, Nestor told us. With the help of his family and
George's, Nestor was working through his grief as well as
could be expected. But I could tell from Nestor's voice over
the phone that he was having a very difficult time.

There had been one more loss for Nestor. On the morning
after George died, Nestor had found the yellow canary dead
on the floor of her cage.

"George loved that bird," Nestor said weakly. "I'm sure he
took her with him."

Michael Keith

My beautiful, talented, imaginative and loyal friend Eve.
She spent a year and a $50,000 inheritance in Key West,
in search of a perfect romantic fit.

Adam Met Eve
on a Saturday Night

E ve visited Key West for the first time with her mother. She'd just completed work on a masters degree in fine arts. She was 30 years old. At the motel she caught the eye of Adam, the pool boy. He invited Eve out for coffee, then out for dinner, and finally, back to his room. Adam was her age, and had a masters degree, too. She was smitten, with him, with his island, and with thoughts of making major changes in her life.

Upon arriving back at her home up north, Eve learned that she'd inherited money. It seemed that fate was shoving her out of the gloom and into the sunshine. As she packed for the move she phoned Adam frequently, to discuss island living. With conversation, they forged a sweet connection.

A month before the move, Eve flew down to rent an apartment. That's when I met her. She was bright, hip and very funny. Over the first of many lunches and dinners we would share, Eve described her great expectations for her new life in

Key West. She told me about Adam. In every way that mat-
tered, Eve said, they fit. But Adam wasn't looking for a perfect
fit. Not yet, anyway. He'd told Eve he wouldn't marry until he
was 40, and that he very much enjoyed being free.

I told Eve I hoped she wasn't moving to the last resort with
the hope of turning her sexy tourist hustler into a mate. She
said she was moving to Key West for the sun. But I know love
sickness when I see it, and Eve had it bad. The move was all
about Adam.

Once she settled into her new nest, Eve scoured the help-
wanted ads. But the jobs she wanted always seemed to fall
through, and the jobs she was offered, she really didn't want.
She stayed unemployed.

Meanwhile, Adam's affections waxed and waned. When he
was sweet and attentive, Eve believed he felt as ardently about
her as she did about him. When he seemed distant, she felt
betrayed and injured. When she felt hurt, Adam comforted
her, which reinforced her belief that he was really in love. The
terrible cycle of hope and disappointment wore her down,
and before a year was up, Eve collapsed into a terrible depression. Her parents showed up, packed up her things, and
whisked her back home.

That was two years ago. Now, Eve is her bright, funny self
again. She lives up north. She has a great job. Recently, she
came for a visit. Over dinner she told me she still entertains
thoughts of returning to Key West, and of making it work this
time. She has unfinished business here, she said, and was
longing for closure with Adam. She had tried unsuccessfully
to locate him, but didn't even know if he still lived on the
island.

Just then, in a quirky turn of fate, who in the world but
Adam ambled past the restaurant. Eve ran out and caught up
with him. They chatted briefly, and agreed to meet in a nearby bar in an hour. An hour later, I walked Eve to her ren-

dezvous, but the pool boy was no where to be found. And believe me, we looked for him.

The next day Eve told me that perhaps the universe was showing her that Adam was not a man she could count on. I suggested that Adam himself was showing her that by not appearing for their midnight meeting at the bar. But Eve didn't want to believe that Adam was cruel enough to stand her up.

Unbelievably, Eve ran into Adam once again during her visit. In a coffee shop. She asked him for his e-mail address. He didn't remember it. His phone number? He didn't remember that either. He told her she looked beautiful. (She did.) They said goodbye.

I drove Eve to the airport, anxious to get her out of here before Adam could stomp her heart again. She said she'd always remember Adam as "the $50,000 fling" because that's how much her inheritance had been and she'd blown every penny of it on her year in Key West.

"Trust me, Sister," I told her, in my best Judge Judy accent. "You got off cheap."

Every woman owes it to herself to have at least one very hot affair
with a Cuban man. Love and be loved. Bask in the light of
his sweet and salty Latin gaze. But always, always,
be prepared to let him go.

Donde Tu Vas?

Cuban men love women, unabashedly, unreservedly, and without pretense. You don't have to be a beautiful woman, or a very young one, or a terribly charming one to spark a flame in a Cuban man's eyes. Being female is enough. When a Cuban man gazes unflinchingly into your eyes, he is gazing into the eyes of all womankind, of femininity at large, and of his beloved mother.

Cuban men are funny, sweet, and eternally restless. Possessed of a primeval inner rhythm, they require less sleep than the rest of us, and are constitutionally incapable of staying in one place for long. They are very difficult, and in many cases, impossible to domesticate.

Nonetheless, every woman should have one grand Cuban passion at least once in her life. If you get more than that, you're very lucky or very dumb — or both. My first Cuban heart-throb was Desi Arnez, who played Ricky Ricardo, the smolderingly handsome Latino conga drum player who loved Lucy no matter what she did, in a thousand episodes of *I Love*

Lucy that formed the backdrop of my childhood. Surely millions of little girls just like me grew up in love Desi Arnez.

I discovered Key West while nursing a broken heart, the result of a dead-ended love affair with a swarthy Italian New Yorker who was, and is even more so today, a dead ringer for Fidel. (Perhaps that should have told me something.) But that broken heart was child's play compared to the mother of all heartaches that awaited in the steamy sub-tropics.

I married a Cuban man I first spotted across a crowded room. I'm going to have his babies, I thought, as I admired his stature, his aquiline nose and his dark Spanish eyes. A few years later I did have his baby. Four years after that we divorced. Being a Cuban esposa helped me to grow emotional muscles I never dreamed I had. My Cuban lover left me sadder, but wiser, too. He left my scarred heart as big and strong and sturdy as a long-distance runner's.

Recently a friend in Miami introduced me to her new housekeeper, a woman recently arrived from Cuba, struggling to learn English. I told her, in my bad Spanish, that I'd once been married to a Cuban. She asked me if he'd taught me Spanish.

"His mother taught me to say 'Donde tu vas?' " I told her. "It was all the Spanish I ever needed."

She laughed knowingly, and so did I. It means: where are you going?

Join us on the worldwide web at:
www.JuneKeith.com

*Mikey and Michael on the water in Lunenburg, Nova Scotia.
From the moment his stepfather (Michael Keith) came into his life,
he has been welcoming and respectful.*

Babes in Paradise

Among the questions most often asked of me when I'm waiting on tables is this one: "Is Key West a good place to raise children?" It's not an easy question. I'm really not sure. Sometimes I think it's the best place on the planet to raise kids. Sometimes I think it's the worst.

My son Mikey was born and raised here, and he's a happy little Conch. He seems well adjusted and - what I like best about him - wonderfully honest. But I wonder if he has been too spoiled here. Will the ways of the world that lies beyond the Monroe County line come as a shock to him?

The thought of sending him off to a place like, say, New York City, brings to mind the story of Tarzan the Ape Man - the beautiful, innocent savage who puts on a suit and travels to London only to be hideously misunderstood by genteel society.

Mikey, like all of the Keys kids I know, is beautifully free of prejudice. His mind seems as sunny and open as a perfect day in paradise. How will that big-heartedness play in other, gloomier places?

When Mikey was just 5 years old, he liked playing with GI Joe dolls. He had quite a collection. One day his father noticed him playing with his GI Joes and asked him how things were going with them.

"They're real happy today, Dad," Mikey said.

"Why are they so happy?" his dad asked.

"Because they are getting married!" Mikey answered jubilantly.

"They can't get married, Mikey," his dad said. "They're guys."

"They're gay guys, Dad," Mikey said.

That's the kind of lack of prejudice I'm talking about.

Somehow I can't envision some little kid in Cleveland staging a wedding for his GI Joes. And if he did, I can't imagine his father being very pleased upon hearing about it.

Mikey is equally open-minded about his career possibilities. I recently tried a dusty old piece of homespun psychology on him that my mother used to use on me. When one of his teachers sent home notice that he was slacking off in school, I threatened him with: "Do you want to grow up and wait on tables to make your living?"

"Well, actually I wouldn't mind waiting on tables at all," Mikey answered thoughtfully. "It looks like a lot of fun, and I've heard you say that the pay is better than at any other job you could get in Key West."

After spending a considerable amount of time looking at a museum exhibit of particularly bizarre abstract paintings, Mikey, then 10 years old, astounded me with an amazing insight.

"A lot of people would look at those paintings and say 'What's so great about this stuff? I could do this!' But you know what, Mom?" Mikey said. "They didn't do it. This guy did it." He has always knocked me out with his cool clear vision.

The only poem I ever had published was one about Mikey.

I was paid $15 for it. I used it to buy groceries at Fausto's for dinner.

Mikey's 14 now, and so far, when it comes to being Mikey's mother, I can't seem to go wrong. Maybe, as a psychic told me long ago, Mikey and I really do have a long karmic history. I truly believe that his father and I fulfilled our procreative destinies when we combined our Spanish, Cuban, African, French, English, and Welsh genes to create Mikey. Does this beautiful child of ours deserve anything less than paradise?

What does this mother tell people who ask whether or not Key West is a good place to raise a kid? I tell them it depends on the kid.

A Quiet Kind of Love

I want a quiet
kind of love
A love that's
nice and easy
Not one that
leaves me spinning
off the floor
A quiet kind of love
A love like
Roman candles
I don't think I can
handle anymore

Richard Watherwax

There always comes a time
When love is like a rocket
when it starts the big decline
You've got no way to stop it

I was standing in the ashes
Of the kind of love that crashes
When you soothed me
With your quiet kind of love

*My husband, Michael, wrote this poem for me a couple of months
after we met. Two years later, we married, in the sumptuous
back yard of our good friend, Mayor Richard Heyman.*

No Such Thing as
Too Sweet, Baby

The other night, I had an interesting chat with Gregory - a very good-looking, bright and sensitive man of 26, with whom I work. I was telling Gregory about how wonderful it was to awaken to a stack of gifts and a very sentimental birthday card all from my husband on the morning of my 44th birthday.

"Michael is a very, very sweet man," I said. "Like you."

"Maybe too sweet?" he suggested.

"No such thing as too sweet, baby," I said.

"Doesn't a woman like a man who doesn't make things too easy for her?" Gregory asked. "Maybe a woman your age," I said. "But when a woman gets to be my age, if she's learned anything at all about love, believe me, she'll joyfully settle for sweetness and ease."

When I was 26, I lived for love. I loved dangerous love, the can't-live-with-it, can't-live-without-it kind of love that kept me ever teetering on the brink of self-destruction. Cliff-hanging love was what I wanted, what I craved, what I was willing to go just about anywhere, with just about anyone, to find. I wanted to lie down on the railroad tracks for love. I wanted to walk through hot coals for love. I wanted to feel my heart burn and char in a five-alarm blaze of love. I figured a guy who wouldn't jump off the top of the Empire State Building for love was a cold fish. Him I threw back. I wanted crazy fish, lunatic fish, mad, fat puffer fish, bug-eyed with passion, whose visions of romance were akin to my own.

If my lover dove off the top of the Empire State Building, well, he would insist that I dive, too. And I would have! Because that was true love.

I died many times for love. And when I wasn't dying, I was searching wildly for my next spin around the dance floor of romance. I wanted to do it all over again and again. The launch. The lift-off. The orbit. The inevitable fiery crash. Wow! Love was a blast!

Eventually, I tired of scraping the smoldering pieces of myself off the floor. It became increasingly difficult to put myself back together again after a crash. I was nursing some pretty terrible wounds when Michael came into my life.

"I have a good feeling about us," he said simply that first summer we spent together, as we walked through dusky streets or sipped cappuccino, or sat on a beach watching the stars.

It took me almost a year of sharing easy pleasures to realize that I was in love with him. Love with Michael was gentle, without desperation, quiet and dignified. It was friendly, reasonable, and most amazing of all, it was painless. No wonder it was so difficult to recognize!

Six years ago today I married Michael. I married him because he's a poet and because his eyes are blue like a perfect summer sky. I married him because he's smart and down to earth, and he doesn't talk a lot. I married him because he asked me to. But most of all, I married Michael because he's a very, very sweet man. And at long last I've learned: there's no such thing as too sweet, baby.

June Keith

Wild thing, you make my heart sing.
You make everything groovy.
Sabrina came to Key West for a visit in the winter of 1977.
She stayed for 5 years. Here she is taking my baby Mikey
out for a ride.

The Sleep
of the Fearless

W hen I decided to move to Key West, I invited my most adventurous friend Sabrina to join me. She wouldn't. She wanted to stay in New York City, the place she considered to be the heart of the universe.

I knew I'd miss her, but I was relieved, too, when she decided to stay behind. I was looking forward to hassle-free life in paradise. And although life with the exuberant Sabrina was always fun, it was never quite hassle-free.

A year later, when winter raged up north, Sabrina showed up in Key West. Within days she fell wildly in love with the place and decided to pack up her apartment, come back and stay.

Ever since I was a little girl I had owned a beautiful mahogany blanket chest. When I came south, I couldn't fit it into my Suburu, and so it stayed behind in New York with Sabrina for safe keeping.

When she moved out of her apartment Sabrina and a

helper carried my antique, hand-carved chest down five flights of stairs, placed it on the sidewalk, and went back upstairs for another load. The chest was stolen, at high noon, right off East Seventy-first Street. The loss was a typical occurrence in Sabrina's life. It was also a good example of what happened to things entrusted to her.

Sabrina made a big splash in Key West. She was vibrant, sexy, smart and enthusiastic. I married and became pregnant. The house I shared with my jealous Cuban husband became home base to the foot-loose Sabrina.

Sabrina was an excellent cook who loved baking bread on the rare cool day or roasting a goose or a perfect leg of lamb for a holiday feast. Although she was only 18 at the time, 9 years younger than I, she consistently beat anybody who dared challenge her at Scrabble.

One night Sabrina borrowed the new bike my husband had given me for my birthday. "Don't forget to lock it!" I reminded her. "I won't forget!" she yelled over her shoulder as she pedaled away. "If I lose it I'll owe you a new bike."

She did not lock the bike. It was stolen. And the next day, Sabrina bought me a new bicycle, as promised. But of course the new bike wasn't quite the same as the one my husband had given to me, the one that was gone.

Eventually Sabrina moved on and settled back on the mainland. I confess: I did not miss her. She enrolled in college, then married. She earned a degree to teach, but her first teaching job was only a temporary one. It ended after a year. By then she was divorced, with a baby, taking on series of jobs, none of which particularly interested her.

Five or six years ago, when she was a stockbroker, Sabrina and a friend visited town. They rented a house for the weekend. I advised them to lock the doors and close the windows, but Sabrina laughed off my concerns.

"We're not afraid," she said.

On their second night in town, a thief came in through an open window while they slept, and made off with their money and their credit cards.

Last week I visited Sabrina at her home on Florida's space coast. She lives there because of a custody arrangement. Just out of graduate school, she's scheduled to start a new teaching job this fall. Her house, which she bought with an inheritance, is homey, bright and very comfortable. As the sun slid behind the horizon, Sabrina and I sat and talked on a breezy patio in her backyard. I felt my heart flood with warmth, my love for her rekindled by her fiery brilliance, her seamless charm. We talked until well past midnight.

When we finally decided to go to bed, Sabrina went through the house turning off lights and letting a couple of cats in for the night. She closed, but didn't lock, the front and back doors. I followed behind turning the flimsy locks.

"Still neurotic about security?" Sabrina chided.

"Yeah, I guess so," I admitted. "But I'm still in possession of my cash and my credit cards and my bike."

I retired to the guest room, locked the door, and slept the fitful sleep of the wary, while in another part of the house, Sabrina slept the peaceful sleep of the unafraid.

The quirky art of Patricia Townsend. This one is called
"Titty and the Purple Tights."

The Great Wall

It's rare for a day to pass when I am not asked for directions the Hemingway House, which is located four doors down the street from my own.

The path to Hemingway's House has been beaten smooth by now. You would think the location of the town's most famous tourist attraction would be anything but a mystery, and yet, nearly every time I exit my home I am approached by people who ask in tentative tones, "Is this the way to the Hemingway House?"

We are so close to the place I could almost yell to Larry, my very debonair, snowy-haired friend who works the ticket booth there, "Hey Larry, how are you today?" And he could sing back, "I'm fine, darling! How are you?" And we would each hear the other.

Once I was hired to write a brochure for an English painter named Patricia Townsend who moonlighted as a tour guide at the Hemingway House. I invited her over for dinner, at which time I hoped to get to know her better.

"Can you come at six?" I asked.

"Yes, if the damned tourists don't keep me late asking ridiculous questions about the great Hemingway," she said scornfully.

"What kinds of questions?" I asked.

"Obnoxious ones. They want to know: 'Is this where he shot himself?' and 'Is this where he went to the bathroom?' They're disgusting!"

"So we'll see you around six?" I asked.

"Yes. All right. But tell me, what do you eat? No meat, I hope."

"No," I assured her. "No meat. I'll fix pasta."

"With tomato sauce?" she asked. (She pronounced it toe-maaa-toe.)

"Yes, and lots of garlic," I said. "We love garlic. It discourages the mosquitoes."

"Oh, I can't have garlic! It will carry on my breath when I give tours to the Hemingway fans," she said.

"Fine. No garlic," I said.

"You don't have any animals do you?" she asked.

"No." I said.

"Because I hate the way you Americans go on about your house pets. People go mad for those mangy Hemingway cats. They pick them up and kiss their little faces! I find it utterly appalling! "

"No animals," I said. "But we do have a little boy. Do you like children?"

"Ab-hoooooor them," she said, turning her head as if avoiding a bad smell.

"Oh, I see. Well, perhaps we'd better postpone this visit until my son grows up and goes away to college," I said.

In fact, I never did write that brochure. And Patricia Townsend, who'd hoped to find happiness and artistic success in Key West, was ultimately very disappointed here. Her next move was to Indiana, and that's where she died.

Still, I can't help remembering her feisty spirit when I pass by the Hemingway House. The other day, I was walking by the great brick wall that surrounds the place. I thought of Patricia Townsend, and I also thought of Toby Bruce. Bruce was a childhood friend of Pauline Hemingway's who came all the way from Piggott, Arkansas to build that brick fence. Toby loved Key West. He married a Key West woman, and they lived here for the rest of their lives. Their son, Dink Bruce, lives here still.

"Is Hemingway's house around here?" a woman anxiously asked, breaking into my thoughts.

"It's right here," I said, patting Toby's handiwork. "Right behind this wall that Hemingway had built to keep the tourists out."

Contributed

*The Copa burned to the ground since I wrote this column.
And beautiful Sasha Sterling, shown here striking a dramatic pose,
is dead. And so is Nigel. And so is Steven. All of them are gone
since the wonderful night when we drank and laughed
and swayed to "The Land of Make Believe."*

The Land Of
Make Believe

When I wondered aloud what I should wear to the annual Miss Key West Copa Pageant Thursday night, my husband, Michael, gave me some very good advice.

"Don't try to compete with a bunch of drag queens, honey," he said. "Keep it real simple."

Right. So I slipped into some very basic black went down to watch my second Miss Key West contest with a couple of guys from the restaurant where I work.

Ken Morgan, grill man at the Lighthouse Cafe, costume designer and Copa regular, is a good companion at a drag show. Ken arranged for our stage-side table, introduced me to the Copa's many personalities and patiently answered my innumerable questions about how men create the illusion of glittering feminine beauty, in many cases a lot better than women do, or want to do.

The theme of the Ninth Annual Miss Key West Pageant was

"Land of Make Believe." Get it?

A song by the same name blared over the Copa's industrial strength stereo system as we took our seats.

It's a place where no one cries.

It's a place where no one dies.

And good vibrations always greet you.

"God I love camp," beamed Nigel Greene, a Londoner new to town. "I love the frivolity! The fickleness! Here you can say and do anything you like, and nobody gives a damn."

"So you like the United States?" I asked him

"The States? Not particularly," he answered. "I like Key West."

Finally the five contestants were introduced and arranged on stage, each make-believe doll more gorgeous than the next. In magnificent gowns, jewels and coiffures, they stood smiling radiantly as the judges were introduced. Then, while the contestants rushed backstage to prepare for the swimsuit competition, Judge Sasha Sterling took the stage to lip-synch "It's Great to be Back Among Friends." Moments earlier, I had met Sasha, a personable and dramatically beautiful blond with green eyes and a trim figure. Sasha has won a number of national pageants and is a regular and popular performer on the local as well as national drag scene.

Most recently she'd been crowned First Runner Up in the Miss Gay California Beauty Contest but she had stepped down before the end of her reign she told me, to return to Key West.

As Sasha performed, I glanced around the table and saw that Ken was sobbing silently as he watched her. I looked at Steve.

"She's dying," Steven said, his eyes red with tears.

"No she's not," I said, trying vainly to make a joke. "She's not dying at all. People are loving this!"

"She's been very ill," Steve repeated. 'That's why she came

back to Key West."

Serena Monteil, of Tampa, the eventual winner the pageant, lip-synched to "The Greatest Love," the about learning to love yourself.

Midway through the song, Serena, a sultry Latin with magnificent eyes and perfect teeth, suddenly removed her wig, earrings, her ruffled gown and even her makeup to reveal another part of herself: an impressive looking man in soft leather pants and a silk shirt.

The remarkably graceful transformation, from alluring and feminine to strong, confident and uncompromisingly male - brought the house down.

"My god, he really did it!" Steve yelled to me over the cheers and thunderous applause. "He really got it just right."

June Keith

Rocky says that the ride from Daytona Beach to Key West is one of the most beautiful he's ever taken on his Harley-Davidson – far different from the tree-lined hills and valleys of upstate New York. Rocky quickly made friends during his visit to Key West. I'd hoped he might decide to stay. He would easily blend in with his sweet disposition and open heart. But he prefers to live in New York, where the roads are endless and the hands on the seasonal clock are ever turning.

Hard Rock, Soft Rock

H ere in Key West people don't often cross over to the other side of the street to avoid meeting up with my brother Rocky on the sidewalk. We're tolerant here in paradise.

It's not necessarily that way in other places. Even in New York, which most people probably consider to be a fairly liberal place, Rocky seems to attract a lot of negative attention.

Rocky is a big guy. His hair is long. He doesn't shave. He has several tattoos. One is a snake on his right arm. As a gift on her 40th birthday, Rocky had his girl friend's name tattooed over his heart.

Rocky usually wears jeans, a T-shirt and a leather jacket, or even all leather when he's doing a lot of riding on his Harley. He loves riding his Harley down here in Florida. He says that U.S. 1, between Miami and Key West, is the most breathtaking ride he's ever taken.

I was at work, waitressing at the Lighthouse Cafe, the last time Rocky arrived in town. He came by the restaurant and drank a cappuccino while he waited for me to finish my shift.

After work I introduced my brother to my fellow workers. There were five or six of them sitting around a table in the dining room. Most of them are gay.

"This is my brother Rocky," I said. "Rocky, this Dougie, Nikki, Steven, Raymond, Will and Robert.

"Which one these fairies are you going to be up first, Rocky?" I joked.

Rocky laughed. In spite of his burly looks, Rocky is as sweet and soft as a puppy. In the days and nights that followed, Rocky and I rode the trolley, wandered up and down Duval Street and watched the sun set. I introduced him to lots of island people.

"I feel different about gay guys after being here," Rocky told me a few days into his visit. "I used to think gay men were creepy - but your friends really great."

One night Rocky came into the Lighthouse with a bunch of biker friends from New York. They, too, sported lots of long hair, beards, tattoos and leather.

Like Rocky, they looked kind of scary. I noticed several customers casting worried looks their way. In fact, the bikers were courteous and surprisingly low key. They tipped well, too.

Most of Rocky's biker friends, like him. are garbage men. Many are employed by the City of New York Department of Sanitation. They make plenty of money and earn lots of vacation days, which they use for travel. They are passionate about riding America's highways on their Harley-Davidsons. They don't appear to get particularly fired up about much else. Their lives seem uncomplicated, enviably simple.

On the last night of Rocky's visit, he came alone to the Lighthouse for dinner. He was invited by a couple of off-duty waiters and some of their friends to dine with them. Rocky sat at the head of the table, grinning and sipping Budweisers like a blissed-out Buddha. The conversation rolled around to

Rocky's size and obvious strength. How strong was he?

To demonstrate, Rocky picked Dougie up over his head in a neat shoulder press. Amazed, Will asked to be similarly lifted. Rocky, the gentle giant, complied happily.

Last week Rocky sent photos of his new house covered in snow after the recent blizzard in New York. I took them to work to show the guys.

"Do you remember Rocky?" I asked Dougie.

"Of course I do," Dougie said. "Rocky changed my life. Before I met him, I thought bikers were creepy. But now I that I know Rocky, I know bikers can be great people - like him."

Rocky Mazza

*Self-portrait in a doorway. My brother Rocky, surrounded
by his favorite things: fishing rods, electric bass, oil painting
of himself by a onetime girlfriend, and a cigar box of family pictures.
The tax man told Rocky that this house, where he lived for several
years, was the smallest occupied dwelling in Westchester, New York.*

The Windchill Factor

I was watching the weather channel when my brother Rocky phoned from up north. The scene on my TV screen was pretty bleak. The reporter's breath condensed in great foggy clouds around her face each time she spoke, as she described the massive snowstorm battering New York City. Behind her, snow was falling like crazy. Pedestrians were slipping and sliding. Taxis were colliding. Schools were closing. Airports were shutting down.

"Wow! The weather's pretty terrible up there, huh?" I said to Rocky, who lives 50 miles north of the city.

"Nah," he said, with tough guy nonchalance. "It's not bad."

"It looks like a blizzard on TV," I said.

"Yeah, I guess it is," Rocky said. "Hey, it's Christmas bonus time. I got a bunch of envelopes here I haven't even opened yet."

Rocky is a garbage man, which makes him, employment-wise, the most successful of my siblings. On top of his great salary, each year he collects a small fortune in Christmas tips from his satisfied customers. And each year he calls me on the phone to brag about it.

"Why don't you open up a couple of those envelopes and buy yourself plane ticket and come down for Christmas," I suggested.

"I don't need to open these envelopes to come to Key West," he chuckled.

Last summer when his romance crashed, he decided to move to the Keys, a move he's been seriously considering since the first time he came here years ago. For a time it looked as if he really meant to come. He sold his house. He announced to his boss that he was leaving Westchester and the garbage business. He subscribed to Keys newspapers and began hunting for property.

"I gave my boss a year's notice," Rocky told me.

"You did?" I asked incredulously.

"Yeah. I did," Rocky said. "And he gave me a raise."

Just before he called the other day, I'd mailed a Christmas card to him. In it I asked him why we hadn't heard much from him lately. But I think I know the answer. The last time we talked he said he'd spent Thanksgiving with Kathy, his on-again, off-again girlfriend of 13 years.

"They'll be back together by Christmas," my husband Michael predicted.

"I went hunting last weekend," Rocky told me.

"Did you shoot anything?" I asked.

"Nah. I never shoot anything," he said. "I just like to walk around in the woods. I stayed at Kathy's."

Uh-oh, I thought. But I didn't scold my baby brother for being a fool for love. I'm no one to talk.

"So is it real cold there?" I asked, steering the conversation away from the news I did not want to hear.

"Yeah, and I've been thinking," Rocky said. "It's 27 degrees up here today. With the windchill factor it's like 10 degrees.

And you know what I'm wearing? A T-shirt. And L.L. Bean cotton pants. Green, 'cause it's Christmas."

"If that's what you wear when it's 27 degrees in New York," I said, "what are you going to wear when it's 92 degrees in Key West?"

"See, that's what I'm saying," Rocky said. "I'll have to go naked. I'll have to live on an island and kill my own food."

"You're going to live on lizards and birds?" I asked.

"No. I'm thinking I'll go to one of those monkey islands. Eat monkey meat," he said.

'They're putting them in cages now," I said.

'Then they'll be easier to shoot," he said.

We made a couple of monkey jokes, and then Rocky said, "The house next door to Kathy's is for sale. It's beautiful, on the crest of this woody hill. I can get a real good deal on it."

"What about monkey island?" I asked.

"Well that's just it," he said. "You know I could never kill anything."

Esther's ninth birthday party, 1959. We were best friends.
Esther and I are standing. Sally, seated on the left, is the girl
who dropped the water glass. She died a few years ago, of cancer.
Janet, seated on the right, was our campus queen during senior year.
She died when we were 22 years old, sadly, by her own hand.
Check out those snazzy party dresses! My dress was probably
a hand-me-down from Esther.

My Black History

I was seven years old the first time I saw a person of color. Her name was Esther Moses, and on the day she was introduced to my second-grade class I was immediately awed by her brown skin, her black hair in many braids, her liquid eyes, and her terrible shyness. As soon as I could, I rushed over to her and offered to be her friend.

I had recently arrived in Westchester County, New York, from Nova Scotia, and felt very much an outsider. Esther had just moved to the area from New York City. Her home, which I visited often, was far more opulent than any I had ever seen. There was a swimming pool, the first one I'd ever seen, and the first one in our country town, in which I spent many happy summers. The house had been built by Esther's father, a wealthy businessman who lived in Harlem. Mr. Moses visited on Sundays. He arrived in a Lincoln Continental, driven by a timid chauffeur unaccustomed to winding country roads. Sometimes, Mr. Moses took us to church in his car. The chauffeur would accelerate, brake, accelerate, and brake, and we'd ride jerkily along. Mrs. Moses sat between Esther and me in the back, to monitor our behavior, but try as we might, none of us in the back seat could help giggling at Mr. Moses's chauffeur.

Mrs. Moses was a magic woman, with island roots and a mysterious accent. She was ever busy cooking or cleaning or ironing Esther's fine clothes. There was a chicken coop in the back yard - another first for the area, and probably illegal. She slaughtered her own chickens. She introduced my family and me to okra and grits and rice. Her conversation was punctuated with many modulating "mmmm-mmm's." She was affectionate and lavish with her hugs and kisses.

I went to New York City for the first time on a train with Mrs. Moses and Esther. We stayed in Harlem with Mrs. Moses's sister. We shopped in the outdoor markets of Spanish Harlem and I delighted in hearing Spanish being spoken and in seeing nothing but black people for as far as I could see. Once, it occurred to me that being the only white person in a sea of what were then called colored people was how Esther felt back home in Westchester, where she was the only colored person in a sea of whites. It was a happy observation. I fell in love with the city, and my many weekends there with the Moses. Esther lives in New York City with her husband and two sons still.

We went to Radio City Music Hall for movies and the Rockettes. Mrs. Moses always sat between Esther and me. When a scene came up in a film that she considered too racy for us, she pulled our heads into her chest to prevent us from seeing it. Our heads bumped, and we giggled. Esther balked at her mother's over-protectiveness. I didn't. I welcomed any opportunity to nuzzle against Mrs. Moses, to feel safe, and to breathe deeply of her wonderful, powdery fragrance.

Esther came to my house, too. One day we visited a classmate who lived in my neighborhood. Sally served us Cokes.

Then, she dropped the glass Esther had drunk from on the floor, shattering it. I sensed something sinister in the gesture.

At the bus stop the next morning, I asked about the broken glass. Sally said that it had been no accident, that she had purposely broken the glass because no one in her family wanted to drink from the same glass a colored person had.

I'd immigrated to America from a remote mining town in Canada, I'd been to Harlem, and Radio City Music Hall, and been driven to church in a chauffeured limousine. I loved, and was loved, by people both black and white. And throughout all that, I had lived innocent of racism. Then a girl named Sally, who'd never been anywhere, lobbed bigotry into my world like a hand grenade.

Forty years later I still remember the way I felt when Sally told me that. I was surprised. Then, somehow ashamed. But finally, I was sorry for Sally. I pitied her, because in her world, there was no magic island woman to love her, and feed her okra and gingered chicken, and take her to Harlem, and show her the beautiful, flip side of her white universe.

*Joe Savago's hero,
President John F. Kennedy
in Key West with
British Prime Minister
Harold Macmillan,
1961.*

John F. Kennedy Library

Joe's yearbook photo and caption —1966

JOSEPH E. SAVAGO
Joe was a National Merit
Semifinalist . . . winner
of N.C.T.E. ... Editor and
co-founder of the Jay Blade ...
Telluride Summer Program
at Princeton last summer ...
Dislikes narrow-minded
people ... plans to become
a college professor.

*Sometimes I dream that Joe Savago is coming to Key West.
In my dream I make plans. I know he'll love it here. This place
was made for people like Joe. It's full of broad-minded people.
I'll walk him through the Presidential Gates at the foot of Caroline
Street. Late at night we'll hang out at a wine bar, smoke cigarettes
and compare notes on memories of John Jay High School.*

Rebel Joe & JFK

In the fall of 1960 Joe Savago sported a Kennedy-for-President sticker on the spine of his loose leaf notebook while the rest of us were shamelessly wooed by Nixon Republicans who drove up and down the streets of South Salem, New York, handing out cheery red-white-and-blue straw hats. We kids loved those hats and became Nixon supporters the minute we put them on our heads.

But not Joe Savago. Even at 12, Joe had a mind of his own. Perhaps he was the only Kennedy man in the neighborhood because he was Catholic, or maybe he was an intellectual. Whatever the reason, Joe was used to being different.

Joe was a moody rebel. Later, when we got into high school, I remember watching him on a hundred mornings, flick his cigarette butt into the snow as the school bus pulled up and unfolded its doors before him. I watched hopefully as Joe climbed wearily bus.

I always hoped that Joe would sit next to me, and often, he did. While other kids considered Joe to be a square, I thought he was tremendously cool, sexy, remote. I adored him and our early morning chats - though Joe was wildly sophisticated, two years older than I.

Joe eventually went to college on a slew of scholarships. In the summer of his junior year, Joe went on a hitchhiking tour of Europe.

One August day, the headlines in the local paper screamed the heart-breaking news of Joe Savago's death. He'd been hit by a car in Germany. Only his passport identified Joe's badly mangled body, which was sealed into a coffin and shipped home. On the Saturday they buried him, Joe's parents returned home to find a letter from him in their mailbox. It was postmarked two days after the date of his death. Joe wrote that his back pack and his identification been stolen. Sure enough, the body buried that morning did not belong to Joe but to a soldier gone AWOL who had stolen Joe's identity.

The newspapers went crazy, telling the weird tale of Joe Savago's death and subsequent rebirth, spinning it a dozen different ways, always noting Joe's magnificent academic career.

A few weeks later we sat in schoolmate Eric Kaye's living room talking with Joe, who'd become something of a celebrity. He sucked away on his Camel cigarettes, mulling the irony of reading of his own death.

"Everybody asks me if I'm going to write a book about this," Joe said haughtily. "Of course I'm not!"

And I wondered, why not? But Joe remained a mystery to me as he floated away from my life and I wandered ever farther from New York.

In 1985 Eric Kaye visited me in Key West. We talked about the old neighborhood - who'd gone where, done what, and so on. I asked Eric about Joe Savago. "Joe Savago died," Eric said.

"Again?" I said, trying to laugh as a molten heaviness crushed my heart.

"He died of AIDS a couple of years ago," Eric said sadly. "What a waste."

Today my memories of Joe Savago are jumbled into the same category as the John Kennedy ones. Bright lights snuffed too soon. Brilliant but doomed. All that stuff. I wonder if Joe Savago knew he was destined to die young.

On the afternoon that President Kennedy died, I sat next to Joe on the school bus home. My eyes were stinging from an hour of tears. My head was aching from the strain. I waited for Joe to say something about how stupid it all was, to somehow release the terrible tension. But he didn't say a word. He just sat there, clutching his books in his lap, and staring silently out the window into the bleak November day.

Stuart and me. All grown up.

Forever Stuart

In the final scene of the great film *Pee Wee's Big Adventure*, Pee Wee tells his friends that he doesn't need to pay particular attention to his life story reenacted on the big movie screen. Why not?

"Because," he says, "I lived it." Then he prances off into the night.

That's how I felt when I saw the play *Forever Plaid*, written by my old high school buddy, Stuart Ross.

In high school, Stuart Ross was a nerd. Glasses. Braces. A tad chunky. He was in the honors class, an insular group of overachievers with big IQs and proportionately small social skills. I was a member of that group of social retards, too, though my scholastic track was pretty hopelessly derailed the first time I heard Jim Morrison sing "Break On Through to the Other Side."

Meanwhile, Stuart's interests remained wildly out of sync with the generational madness of the '60s. In or out of school he wore khaki pants, button-down shirts and sensible shoes.

He played the trombone in the school band. While the rest of us were saving up for the next Rolling Stones album, Stuart was carefully mapping out his career in serious showbiz.

He was a member of the drama and the audio-visual clubs. In a variety show he sang "Pardon Me Miss, But I've Never Been Kissed by a Real Live Girl," with such conviction and charm, you'd think he'd been born backstage at the thousandth performance of *Little Me*.

In spite of his nerdy ways, I liked Stuart. But it was through show tunes that we became real friends. He and his girlfriend, Ellen, introduced me one day to the music from *The Fantastiks*. I was so smitten, I rushed out after school to buy my own copy of the album.

A small clique of *Fantastiks* lovers grew at our high school. And the next year our school play was, guess what? *The Fantastiks*, with Stuart and Ellen in the lead roles.

I did not see Stuart again for many years. Then, around 1983, he showed up in Key West. He'd just graduated from EST training. I'd just become divorced. We met for cocktails at the Monster Bar. He moved into my house that afternoon, and spent the next few weeks typing furiously at my kitchen table, and conversing frequently with his agent in New York. Then, he disappeared from my view once again.

In 1990, I got a phone call from Stuart.

"June, I've got a hit!" he said. And he did. His show *Forever Plaid* was packing them in off-Broadway, and Stuart was suddenly a star. Writer. Director. Choreographer. An overnight success in, as he put it, "only 15 years, 7 weeks and 3 days!"

"I'm making lots of money," he said in an infrequent phone call several years later, "but I don't really have time to spend it. Crazy, huh?"

When *Forever Plaid* came to Miami's Coconut Grove Playhouse, Stuart invited me to opening night. What a thrill! At the cast party, he introduced me to his friends, saying "In high school June and I were the dumb kids in the smart group."

Later, as we drove along Miami Beach in his rented Lincoln Continental, Stuart told me how proud he was of me, and how impressed he was with my happy life in Key West. My husband. My son. My little Conch house.

"But I'm still a loser," I said, in a fit of self-pity over my lack of artistic success. "I still feel like the dumbest kid in the smart group. "

"You'll always feel that way," Stuart laughed. "But don't you see, June? That's what *Forever Plaid* is about. It's about you and me and other people like us. The kids in the audio-visual club. The ones who auditioned for every school play and never got to play the lead. The four-part harmony groups who wanted just once to sing on a stage and get paid for it.

It's about people like us, the ones who never learned to stop dreaming. "

Andy Neuman

*The annual Hemingway Look-Alike Contest at Sloppy Joe's
anchors a week-long Hemingway Days Festival celebrated
in Key West each July. During Hemingway Days you see dozens
of older white-haired guys with big bellies, walking the sidewalks,
eating in the restaurants, and shopping in the Salvation Army
Thrift Shop for white cable-knit wool turtleneck sweaters like
the one Hemingway wore in an apparently widely distributed
promotional photo taken in the '50s. Obviously, that photo
was not taken in Key West.*

Uncle Jack

H e wasn't my uncle, but I wished he was. In my mind I called him Uncle Jack. There were always kids around Jack. They were his own kids, assorted nieces and nephews, their friends, foster kids and Jack's friends' kids. I was a neighbor. Jack's wife Audrey and my mother were best friends.

Jack worked in education, first as a teacher, then as a guidance counselor, and finally, as principal of a huge city high school. Week nights he attended endless meetings. Usually he missed supper. Eventually, he was only available to his family and friends on weekends and school vacations.

Summers, Jack was head counselor at a country club day camp. Winter weekends he ran a ski school at a local slope. For the entire length of my New York childhood, a week seldom passed when I didn't participate in some athletic event supervised by Jack. From him I learned to swim, ski, hike mountains and pack a lunch for 15 people.

Every summer we all piled into two or three station wagons

and drove north for a week on the beach in Maine, followed by a week of camping in the mountains in Jack's home state of New Hampshire.

Jack, always the only adult male in the group, was our leader. He smoked a pipe, was always in motion, and never seemed to run out of enthusiasm or patience.

Eventually, of course, we kids grew up. Jack spent more time on school business, and less and less time at home. Without kids to supply rhythm or reason to their lives, Audrey and Jack divorced.

Then, two years ago, and a quarter of a century since we last threw a football on Old Orchard Beach, Jack phoned me from his apartment in Tampa.

"I'm coming down for the Hemingway Look-Alike Contest!" Jack said happily.

A week later, I picked him up at the airport. He wore baggy khaki pants, and heavy, black lace-up boots. The pants hid metal braces that enabled him to use his legs. Nonetheless, he seemed to walk by lurches rather than by steps. My mother had warned me that his health had deteriorated. He had developed diabetes. His hands shook.

The powerful, red-headed god of my childhood had become a pale and pudgy old man, with wispy hair and beard an odd mixture of faded red and white. The one-time god said he couldn't get a job. Anywhere.

"When I win this contest I'll get lots of good publicity out of it," Jack explained. "People seem to think that a guy 65 years old doesn't have anything to offer. But I still need to work!"

My heart ached as I watched Jack climb onto the stage at Sloppy Joe's Bar for the first round of the look-alike contest. The temperature must have been over 100 degrees. Jack sweated profusely in his Hemingway look-alike sweater.

"I'm not nervous," he announced cheerfully the rowdy

crowd. "I have neuropathy. That's why I shake like this."

To my amazement (he looks nothing at all like Ernest Hemingway) Jack became a finalist and was invited to return the following evening for the final round of the contest.

The next morning we ate breakfast downtown. Jack, now confident of winning the contest, spotted another look-alike finalist across the room and demanded: "Now who looks more like Hemingway? Me, or that guy over there?"

The unspoken answer was: That guy over there.

That night, I could not bear to watch Jack compete. The scene was too hot, too sad and too desperate. I drove him down to Sloppy Joe's and came back home. Then, I told my husband Michael about how strong Jack had once been, and how beautiful the world had looked from the top of Mount Washington, when I was 15 years old and Uncle Jack was my hero.

Contributed

Richard Heyman (left), founder of the Gingerbread Square Gallery,
and two of his most famous, and most troublesome, artists:
Tennessee Williams, in a zodiac shirt, and Henry Faulkner,
who lived with a goat named Alice. Henry taught Tennessee
to paint in exchange for poetry lessons.

Fairy in a Wicker Chair

On the eleventh anniversary of the death of Tennessee Williams, I had breakfast with Richard Heyman and Dr. Lee Dodez at Bogart's Restaurant. Bogart's occupies a building that once housed a restaurant and bar called Claire, which was one of Williams' favorite hang-outs.

I steered the conversation around to the old days and Tennessee Williams. My favorite story is about Tennessee Williams the painter, and his outrageous friend, artist Henry Faulkner. Richard and Lee started the Gingerbread Square Gallery 20 years ago, at 903 Duval Street. There is a Mexican restaurant and bar in that building today. The original gallery was an oddly arranged series of rooms, its walls hung with works by local artists John Kiraly, Sal Salinero, Anne Irvine, Donna Hayes, and Henry Faulkner.

But the Gingerbread's most famous artist in those days was not famous for his painting at all. He was Tennessee Williams, the great playwright. Under the tutelage of his good friend Faulkner, Williams painted his primitive images in dreamy pastels. Each painting was given an exotic name like "Fairy in a Wicker Chair," "Great Silence of the Storm," "Many Moons Ago," "Recognition of Madness," and "Abandoned Chair Occupied Briefly."

Nobody ever said that Tennessee Williams was a great painter, but he was certainly recognized as a literary giant. Some critics believed that Williams' paintings and drawings were new expressions of his genius and therefore significant treasures. His paintings and sketches sold, too, and brought Williams fresh recognition and respect from new sources: art collectors and and art magazines.

The '70s, Williams' biographers all agree, were not easy times for America's greatest living playwright. Williams had grown mistrustful. He was suspicious and constantly wary of people seeking to take advantage of his fame and fortune.

In the late '70s, Richard agreed to help raise funds for the Old Island Restoration Foundation by auctioning off a parcel of works donated by local artists at a gala event. Like all of the other Gingerbread artists, Tennessee Williams readily agreed to donate a piece to the cause. But, to Richard's chagrin, he left town a few days before the event. Hours before the auction was to begin, Faulkner delivered Williams' contribution. It was a pudgy pencil-drawn cherub with Williams' familiar signature "TW" in the lower right-hand corner. The auction went off smoothly and raised plenty of cash for the happy folks at the foundation. Lee sold the Tennessee Williams drawing to a couple from Miami who were thrilled to get it for $750. And that, everybody thought, was the end of that.

A few days later, Williams stormed into the Gingerbread Square Gallery to confront Richard. He had returned to Key West to read in local papers of his wonderful generosity and his fine contribution to the auction. Williams was furious because he'd never sent a drawing for the auction at all. He'd forgotten all about his promise to provide a piece of artwork for the fund-raiser. Finally, Richard deduced that the cherub actually had been drawn by Faulkner, who'd forged Williams' initials to it.

It was a fraud, Williams fumed. He wanted it recovered. Richard found the fiasco somewhat amusing, a typical Faulkner prank. But Williams was enraged, inconsolable. In fact, Faulkner, whom Richard describes as an irrepressible imp, was a far more prolific and successful painter than Williams. (Faulkner died in a car crash in 1981, and today his paintings are very valuable indeed.) The disappointed Miamians reluctantly returned the sketch, but not before Richard returned their $750, a loss absorbed by the Gingerbread Square Gallery. Richard gave the recovered piece to the enraged Tennessee Williams and never heard of it again.

Contributed

*Susan's photo of Don Johnson and his girlfriend
Donya Fiorentino gave the Miami model the evidence
she needed to reveal their love affair to the world,
via the Globe, on November 5, 1985.*

My Year of Love With Don Johnson

L ike most great photographers, my husband's daughter Susan is seldom without her trusty camera. For years, she has been carrying that camera on a strap on her shoulder, like some women carry a purse.

Susan's son Kevin has rarely passed a day on this earth that has not been lovingly recorded on film by his watchful and adoring mom. Kevin is a handsome, blue-eyed, three-year-old with white-blond hair shaped into a perfect Dutch-boy hairdo. He is a cheerful and willing subject. He even models professionally.

All this beauty is no accident. Kevin's mom is no slouch in the looks department either. Back when lived in Key West, she modeled for the Peaches Bathing Suit Company.

While working as a waitress at the Pier House Havana Docks Bar, Susan was chosen to appear in a locally produced video of the Jimmy Buffet song "Who's the Blond Stranger?"

Nowadays Susan runs in less stellar circles. She lives in

Charlotte, N.C., with her husband Ben. The couple, who once shared a haunted apartment on Olivia Street, now devote themselves to raising a family and making mortgage payments.

This weekend, Susan, who is six and a half months pregnant, Ben, and their little boy Kevin, arrive in Key West for a sentimental journey back their old playgrounds. Susan is excited about taking Kevin to see dolphin shows, the City Aquarium and the Sunset Pier.

There is an infectious air of fun around Susan. Kevin is a very lucky kid because it seems that whatever Susan does, wherever Susan goes, great adventures seem to plop right into her lap.

Once upon a time, long before Susan ever thought of getting married, she found herself at a chic Miami party with none other than Don Johnson, the sizzling hot star of the television show Miami Vice. Johnson's date was a very young, very beautiful Latin model. The two appeared to be wildly in love.

Naturally, Susan snapped photos.

"If those pictures come out well, will you send me a few of them?" the model asked Susan sweetly.

Meanwhile, Don Johnson, who was apparently seeing the Miami model behind the back of his long time California actress girlfriend, warned Susan to be careful that the photos didn't "fall into the wrong hands."

Back home in Key West, Susan dutifully watched every step of the one-hour photo processing, to ensure that none of the incriminating photos were duplicated. The photos did turn out well, and so, as promised, Susan sent off a batch of them to Johnson's pretty Miami girlfriend.

Several months later, Susan was standing in the checkout line at Fausto's, her arms loaded with groceries, when she spotted a familiar photo on the cover of a tabloid newspaper.

Under the bold headline "My Year Of Love With Don Johnson" was one of the photos Susan had taken of the cozy couple at the party in Miami.

"Oh my God," Susan screamed, covering her mouth and dropping her load of groceries. Gasping in horror, she grabbed the paper from the rack and stared at it incredulously. "Oh no!"

A guy in the next checkout line watched calmly as Susan freaked out.

"What is it with you women and that Don Johnson?" the guy mumbled, shaking his head. "I mean, what the hell do you women see in him?"

June Keith

Bus person Little Stevie, hostess Babs Daitch, bus person English
Mark, and manager Steve Ritchie as they were when we all worked
at the Lighthouse Cafe in 1991. Where are they now?
Little Stevie is around, still adorable, always happy. Babs lives
in Las Vegas and sells cruises. An odd location for a travel agent,
right? English Mark was on his way to the tourist mecca of
Myrtle Beach the last time I saw him. Steve Ritchie, who was
often depressed and rarely satisfied, shot himself in the head
(and died) in 2003. Raymond (not pictured here) became a
Registered Nurse and works at Sloan-Kettering Hospital
in New York City.

Bus Person Wanted

We're looking to hire a bus boy at the Lighthouse Cafe. Since I'm the poet and the writer on staff, the job of composing the help-wanted ads, printing the nightly specials in chalk on the blackboard, and other tricky writing assignments, falls to me.

Tuesday night, Raymond and I were on duty.

"You want to help me write the ad for the new bus boy?" I asked him.

"You write the ad and I'll check it when you finish," Raymond suggested.

So I wrote: Downtown cafe wants experienced, industrious, intelligent, attractive, and cheerful bus boy.

Raymond came along minutes later and read the ad over my shoulder.

"You can't say they should be attractive," Raymond said, crossing the word out with his pen.

"Then you can't say they should be intelligent," I said, crossing that word out with my pen.

"Bus boy?" Raymond said, frowning at me. "A woman can bus tables, June. I'm surprised at you! You need to say bus person."

So I changed that, too.

Finally, after long and careful consideration, we shaped our ad into one that was concise and politically correct.

"Raymond," I said, when we'd finished the task of creating our want ad, "do you still want me to work for you Saturday night so you can go to your friend's birthday party?"

"The party's been called off," Raymond said.

"What happened?" I asked.

"It got out of hand," Raymond explained. "See - Ramona invited a bunch of straight people from her office, and Joanne invited me and Ron and some other friends of ours. Then they'd invited too many gay couples and not enough straight couples. And course they had too many gay women right from start because they're lesbians and most of their friends are, too. So they kept inviting more people, trying balance the whole thing out and before they knew it, over 100 people were coming. They live in a tiny Conch house. They don't have the space for a big bash.

"So yesterday Ramona called everybody and them that the party was off. She's going to take Joanne out for dinner on her birthday instead. Just the two of them," Raymond said.

"Whew! Another potential political disaster diverted!" I said.

Later, as Raymond and I were polishing silver I got to thinking.

"You know, Raymond, it's hard to believe we're living in a place known for it's end-of-the-road tolerance, not to mention decadence, living so-called alternative life-styles, and we can barely make a move without worrying about its possible political and social repercussions," I proselytized. "I mean where are heading? This is freedom of expression?"

"Well, let's not worry about all that now, honey," Ray said wearily. "Let's just finish cleaning up and go home."

"Come on Raymond, I want to talk about this. Really, don't you think it's silly?" I argued, gathering steam. "I mean that thing about the party being cancelled, that's nuts! Is every-body that sensitive about their sexual orientation? Is that what defines us? And why can't we say we want an intelligent boy? Or person? We do! We want him or her to be attractive, too. Admit it, Ray. You know we do! Let's get honest."

"You know what, June?" Raymond said, as he leaned over and kissed my cheek. "You're really cute you're mad."

Raymond DePhillips

Jon Hynes and me, celebrating Fantasy Fest.
The theme was Jungle Fever.

Table Near A Waitress

A lot of what I know about waiting on tables I learned from my friend Jon Hynes, waiter extraodinaire. Jon doesn't wait on tables anymore. He burned out a couple of years ago - a common fate of those in the table service game.

The alternative to burnout is automation. A waiter becomes more robotic than human - no expression, no humor, no flinch of distaste at oafish manners or skimpy tips - nothing extraneous or extraordinary. A waitron. The automatic waiter simply performs his duties, regular as a metronome. Jon was never that kind of waiter, and neither am I.

For a few winter seasons Jon and I worked together. As a co-worker and as a waiter, Jon was both entertaining and educational. Jon was everybody's favorite waiter. Aspiring to his obvious stature I watched him closely to learn his trade secrets.

"I always ask my customers where they're from," Jon once told me. "It's a good ice-breaker."

So now I do that, too.

When John announced the specials for the night he always added a funny kicker at the end, so his speech might have gone something like this: "We have wild mushrooms en crout, chicken with leeks and wild mushrooms, and lamb chops with grilled wild mushrooms. Guess the boss got a deal in the market today on wild mushrooms, huh?"

So now I do that, too.

In the event of an error, say he forgot an appetizer and served the salad first, he'd simply serve the appetizer after the salad just as if that was the way things were supposed to go.

Yes, that's how I cover my goofs, too.

When customers asked Jon personal questions - like how long he'd been in Key West, whether he lives here year 'round, and so on - Jon had plenty of stuff to tell them about his adventures as a summertime concert roadie with stars like Jimmy Buffet, the Neville Brothers and Don Henley.

I tell my customers that on my days off I write a column for the *Miami Herald*. Sometimes they believe me. Once I waited on a professor of poetry from Rutgers. I told her that I write poetry, too. The next day we read poetry aloud to each other in the garden of the Duval House. She gave me an impromptu lesson in imagery.

I seem to have the most fun, though, with the subject of where we're all from. If they're from New York, we have something in common. I grew up in New York. If they're from Canada, I can say I'm from Canada, too. I was born in Nova Scotia. If they're from Chicago, or Detroit, or Cleveland, all I have to say is, "Brrrr." They roll their eyes and say, "Oooh, yeah."

The other day I was telling fellow waiter Raymond DePhillips how well I do with the where-you-from? routine. Raymond said he'd tried it, but that he had had trouble coming up with appropriate responses to the answers.

"You relate it to something you know about," I explained.

"For example, the other night I waited on two guys who said they were from Dallas, so I said, 'Hey! I had a mammogram today, and the lady who did it was from Dallas.' "

"I'm just not good at it," Raymond said. "Some people told me they were from Milwaukee, so I thought for a minute and I said, 'Oh, Jeffrey Dahmer!' That wasn't so good."

"You could have said, 'Oh, Laverne and Shirley.'"

One time I told a guy I was from Nova Scotia. He said, "I love that state. It's so beautiful."

"Did you tell him that Nova Scotia isn't a state?" Raymond asked.

"Hell, no," I said. "The customer is always right. I said, 'Yeah, it is a beautiful state, isn't it?' "

Michael Keith

Vic Dunn holds court in a favorite corner of his screen-walled
living room. To his right, a can of beer; to his left, a bottle of
mosquito repellent. Vic told us he liked living on his own private
island just fine. His wife, however, was growing tired of the
dampness and the commute to work. She was ready for a
less-rustic home, with modern conveniences like flushing toilets,
running water, and nearby grocery stores.

Little
Knock 'em Down Key

Rocky, my adventurous brother who lives in New York and dreams of living in the Keys, telephoned the other night. He's come into some money and is looking to buy himself a little piece of Paradise. He called to say he thinks he may have found it in the classified pages of a Keys newspaper.

"It's on an island ten minutes from Summerland Key," Rocky said. "A place with a funny name. You need a boat to get there. Will you check it out for me? Find out where they go to the bathroom."

It made sense that Rocky would be intrigued by visions of on a tropical island far from the hustle and bustle of tourist-swamped Key West. His New York home is on a tree-lined back road, miles from civilization.

Rain fell heavily from low, dark clouds on the Saturday morning my husband Michael and I were scheduled to see Knock 'em Down Key. Just before we left our house in Key

West, the real estate agent, Richard Coarse, phoned to advise us to wear sneakers and long pants. He said he hoped we wouldn't mind "getting a little bit wet."

It didn't seem like a good day for boating, but, encouraged by Richard's enthusiasm, we headed out into the downpour. The rain stopped and the sun began to appear by the time we found the Galley Grill on Summerland Key and waited by the door for our ride out to the island.

Had we launched from the other side of Summerland, explained our navigator Vic Dunn, it really would have taken only 10 minutes to get out to Little Knock 'em Down, just like the ad said. But we were taking the long way around. which meant we motored through a mile or so of canals before we reached the open ocean. Either way, the cost of hiring Dunn's flat-bottomed skiff for the round-trip to tour the island was $25.

"You eliminate a lot of curiosity seekers that way, Coarse explained, as we climbed out of the skiff and onto the island. The tide was low, so we didn't get wet after all.

The quiet on Little Knock 'em Down Key was velvety soft. Almost eerie. Dunn, our navigator, turned out to be the owner of the place. He's 68 years old, and has lived on the island for 18 years. He'd live there longer were it not for his wife's disenchantment with island dwelling.

He hastened to add that she had been a darn good sport all these years. The house, with its screened walls and odd collection of mix-and-match furniture, was neat as a pin, something like a well-organized campsite. In the kitchen, pots and pans hung neatly from a shelf over a kitchen sink, into which the only available water came from huge plastic barrels of collected rain water.

Through the years, Dunn said, he'd dreamed up lots of ways of making the place more cushy, but somehow he'd never gotten around to most of them. A bigger generator would be nice. The 3,600-watt generator there now makes too much noise. But big generators require lots of gas, he said, and he didn't like the idea of paying for, or hauling, all the fuel it would require.

"What about plumbing?" I asked, as we sat in a sitting room and watched brilliantly colored birds darting in and out of a feeder a few feet away.

"Why? Do you have to go?" Dunn asked. 'There's a bucket right outside the back door if you do."

"What about the cold?" Michael asked, warily eying the walls of screen. "It must get cold out here in the winter. "

"Sure it does," Dunn said, chuckling. "You layer lots of clothes on when it's cold."

Living on an island, he said, is a lot like living on a farm. There are many chores to do. The life ain't easy, but it will keep a man in shape, Dunn said.

"Say you need a piece of parsley for cooking," he said. "You've got to get yourself ashore, go to a store, buy what you need, get it back to the boat, motor it back out to the island, walk it up to the house. And that's before you even begin to use it."

Dunn's place, on the market for two months now, is a turnkey sale. Everything you see on the island stays on the island. Even the cats, who darted off like wild animals at the sight of us.

"They're not used to seeing anyone else around here but wife and me," Dunn explained.

The tide had risen by the time we headed back down the to the boat. We soaked our shoes, and the bottoms of our jeans. We laughed a lot on the way back to Summerland, imagining how it might be to live out there.

"So what do I tell Rocky?" I asked Michael, as we headed back to Key West.

"Ask him if he wants to go halves on the place," Michael said.

Richard Wetherwax

"Roy's Dead Now" an evocative portrait of Roy Passwater,
a homeless Key West man, was painted by artist Martin Laessig.
It was hung in the Full Moon Saloon on the day it opened in
the spring of 1977. The Full Moon closed its doors forever
in the summer of 1993. Oh, what a party it was!

The Dark Side
of The Moon

When I read in the paper that the Full Moon Saloon was closing its doors for good, I felt as if I were reading the obituary of an old friend, a wild old friend with whom I'd been in lots of trouble.

True, I hadn't been in the place for years. Nonetheless, I'm sure I'd fulfilled my quota of lost weekends there and certainly qualified as a bonafide "Full Moonie."

I quit the place because I quit drinking, and though it was always a fun place to eat a fish sandwich or make a midnight rendezvous, none of that felt the same as it once had without a couple of the house's overly generous cocktails to guide you round the dark side of the Moon.

But sobriety isn't the only thing that has kept me away from the Moon. Some of the darkest moments of my life happened there.

My first marriage ended at the Full Moon eleven years ago. The comedy team of Mac and Jamie was performing that night, and my husband and I had gone there to celebrate our fourth wedding anniversary. I wanted to see the show, but the waitress told us it was sold out.

"Sorry, honey," my husband said, as if he meant it.

Victor Lathem, one of the owners of the place heard that we, two of the Moon's most dedicated patrons, wanted tickets to the show. He came to table and offered us a couple of tickets as an anniversary gift.

"No thanks," my husband said. "See, I'm expecting a phone call. We gotta get home."

It was a lie. There was no phone call expected and I knew it. Anger sizzled through me like an electric shock.

"That's it," I said evenly, not quite believing the words suddenly flowing from my mouth.

"I want a divorce. "

"Don't say it if you don't mean it," he said evenly.

I meant it. Two weeks later I moved out of his house.

Eventually I found a new lover. He managed a theater and told me how much he despised working with the actors there. He angrily described them as childish and self-centered.

One night he phoned me to break a date we'd made earlier that day. He said he had to work through something with the actors. My roommate and I walked over to the Full Moon for a late supper. And there, holding the hands and gazing deeply into the eyes of one of those childish self-centered actresses about whom he'd complained so bitterly, sat my overworked lover.

He never saw me standing there. He never saw me crying into my Caesar Salad. In fact, he never saw me again.

I was thinking about those sad moments last night, when my husband Michael, his buddy Chuck Krumel and I drove past the darkened Full Moon Saloon. We'd just had a great dinner at El Siboney, and were full of good cheer.

"Boy oh boy, I raised a lot of hell in that place," I said. "And now it's closed."

"They had to close," Chuck said. "All of their customers are either in jail or in recovery!"

"Maybe AA could move into the building," I said. And we laughed.

I told them about the night I decided to divorce my first husband. The memory just didn't seem very sad anymore. It just seemed awfully long ago.

"He wouldn't even see Mac and Jamie with me!" I told Chuck. "He wouldn't even let me laugh. Then, I met Michael, and when Mac and Jamie were at the Pier House I asked to go and see the show. He said 'Sure. Let's have some laughs.'

"So, I married him!"

I was sitting in the back seat, and I couldn't see Michael's face, but I knew he was smiling as he drove our car down Simonton Street and I watched the Full Moon disappear into the darkness.

Sophie Greene

On the night before they left Key West, Martin and Sara
and Michael and I drove up to Sugarloaf Key for dinner
at Mangrove Mama's. The February sky was brilliant with stars.
We stood beneath them, awestruck, and gazed up at the
endlessly vast universe that we share.

Aching for Love

Sara Schwartz and Martin Saxon eloped to Key West this week. They married Friday at noon, in a brief wedding ceremony held in a weather worn gazebo located in the heart of Old Town. Sara's wedding dress was white linen. The day was bright and balmy. The wedding, though simple, was as elegant as any imaginable.

Sara and Martin arrived Tuesday night. They're staying with their friend (and mine) Nigel Greene. They're from London, as is Nigel. Like Nigel, Sara and Martin are very clever, very charming.

Martin owns a trendy Soho restaurant called The Lexington. Sara arranges culinary holidays in Italy. Two years ago Martin spent a week learning about the culinary charms of Northern Italy. He met Sara there. Last fall Martin proposed. They decided to marry in the same place they met, La Camilla, Italy. But Sara was married before and cannot be officially wed in an Italian Catholic Church. Hence the elopement.

The Italian wedding is still on, and all of Martin's and Sara's families and friends will be there. But that's scheduled for this summer. The Key West wedding is the legally binding one.

Wednesday morning we met for breakfast at the Blue Heaven. Sara and Martin had just come from the Monroe Country Courthouse where they'd bought, for $64.50, a marriage license.

The Londoners were surprised and amused with the informal atmosphere at the courthouse. One lady read horoscopes aloud from the newspaper to another lady as several others chatted uninhibitedly on telephones.

Sara offered to show her passport to clerk Elsie Freeman, who said that it was unnecessary.

"When you sign this paper," Elsie explained. "you're saying that everything else you told us is true."

"We'd heard that you Key West people were very laid back," Martin chuckled.

Over breakfast, we discussed wedding locations. Nigel suggested Ft. Taylor Beach. Martin said it was too ordinary. Mallory Pier at sunset? Too tacky. Sara imagined a garden, a sunny church, or an outdoor cathedral.

From a pay phone I called Joe, a wonderful man I know who has a huge, lovely garden behind his home on Petronia Street. Joe, whose favorite city is London, told me to bring the wedding party right over.

"Please find out from Joe what we can do repay his wonderful kindness," Martin said to me.

"Tell them to be happy," Joe said.

By Wednesday night no clergyman had been found who was willing to marry the foreigners without religious, pre-marital instruction. So Martin turned to the Yellow Pages and located two notary publics who perform weddings. The first charges $50. The second performs a spiritually-themed, 20-

minute ceremony for $100.

'Too pretentious," said Sara.

Thursday afternoon, after word of the need for notary public got around town, a woman named Melody was found. Sara and Martin liked her right away and recruited her.

Thursday night, the eve of Sara and Martin's wedding, we met at the top of the La Concha Hotel to watch the sun go down. I'd forgotten how magnificent the island looks from 7 stories up, when the sun is just setting. Dots of light began to sparkle all over the harbor and city below. It was achingly romantic.

Sara and Martin, having settled the wedding plans, were serene and happy, their faces glowing from an afternoon at the beach. All that was left to do for the remainder of the night was look forward to the wedding.

Nigel turned his face toward the harbor and sighed heavily.

"Oh! I wish I was in love!" he cried into the wind and the setting sun.

Tom Netting

Richard A. Heyman
April 3, 1935 - September 16, 1994

Sweet Dreams, Big Daddy

L ast Saturday Richard Heyman decided to forgo another trip to the hospital - the ventilator, the round-the-
clock nurses, the bright lights and the nonstop action.
The hospital might pull him out of his third bout of pneumonia, his doctor told him. But Richard was getting awfully tired
by then. So he decided to stay home.

He's been dealing with HIV for almost 5 years. He's been
damned sick, though often hearty enough in looks and
actions to fool lots of people, for the past two years. He's been
at death's door twice before and miraculously found his way
back both times.

Last Saturday Richard said he'd realized that he didn't
have another recovery left in him. And so Annie, the Hospice
nurse, came. She set up her supplies and got John Kiraly,
Richard's partner, to sign the papers placing her in charge of
Richard's care. Richard is terminally ill. There will be no more
miraculous recoveries.

That evening, family and friends began to arrive. They came from Ohio, Indiana, Texas and Ft. Lauderdale. When they reached Richard's bedside they found him breathing oxygen, resting comfortably, and happy to see them.

By Sunday, he was still comfortable but, ever the congenial host, he'd begun to worry. So many people had been called with the news of his imminent demise. He didn't want to let them down when they'd traveled so far to be with him. What if these weren't his final days?

"Are we rushing you?" I asked him.

"No, but what if this goes on for five weeks?" he asked.

I knew it wouldn't. His comfort and his serenity are testaments to Annie's fine nursing, but Richard was losing strength. Each day, when I put my hand in his, Richard's grip felt perceptibly weaker than it had the day before.

Tuesday afternoon I climbed into Richard's bed and covered his forehead with kisses. I hugged him and tried to make up for all the kisses and all the hugs I won't be giving him when he's gone. He felt warm, and his cheeks were flushed.

"You're my big daddy, and I love you," I told him.

"Oh my!" he smiled. "How in the world did I get so many kids?"

Richard is not my father, of course. I worked for him. He was my boss. He's always been my friend. And to those of us with missing fathers, he feels like a father. I love him like a father.

Wednesday it rained all day. I had work to do, and though I could barely see my way clear of the thick grief that surrounded me, I decided to get to it. All day long people phoned to ask about Richard. I went to the store, and people asked me about Richard. Wherever I went, people wanted to know, how is Richard doing?

By Thursday, Richard had begun to weaken quite visibly. He'd grown pale. His breathing had become more difficult. It was decided that his sedation would be increased to keep him comfortable. His battle with pneumonia was about to end. Around 2:30 that afternoon we were advised by Annie to say whatever last words we had for him.

"Everybody is asking about you," I told Richard when my turn came to speak to him for the last time."

"Oh yeah?" he joked. "What do they want to know?"

They want you to know how much they love you," I said, struggling to stay bright and calm. "They want you to know they are hoping and praying for you to have a safe trip."

His eyes closed and he smiled faintly. He was still wearing his glasses.

"Do you want me to take those glasses off?" I asked.

He nodded. Gently, I took the glasses from his face. I put them on a cluttered table next to his bed, and I left.

Mick Martin

Key West or Bust! After 22 summer vacations in Key West,
our friend Thea finally bought this little conch house next door
to ours. She hopes to retire here some day. Meanwhile, she spends
each precious summer day she can in her tropical retreat,
and dreams of a year-round future in Paradise.

81 Days in Paradise

This morning my summertime friend and neighbor Thea is waking up in a motel in Northern Florida. Today, she'll drive through Georgia, across the Carolinas and into Virginia. Tomorrow, she'll be home in her winter house, and on the day after Labor Day, back in her classroom, fresh and tan after 81 days in Paradise.

Thea's leaving has left me gloomy, just like when I was a kid and Labor Day meant I had to return to the prison of school. Nowadays, Labor Day means losing my girlfriend. When Thea's gone I won't have a pal who lives only a holler through my bathroom window away. I'll miss wandering with Thea through K-Mart on steamy afternoons when it's too hot to stay in the house. I'll miss having a woman my own age to talk to.

But she has to go. To spend 81 days here, Thea must spend 284 days in New Jersey, earning money. Yesterday morning, as I listened to the sound of her securing her house, slamming shut the trunk of her car, and pulling out of the driveway, I did not go to the door to wave goodbye.

Key West isn't a great place for people with abandonment issues. Everyone seems to be leaving, or preparing to leave, or working on finding a way to leave. There isn't enough money here, they say. It's impossible to make ends meet. What? They haven't heard of brown rice and the Salvation Army Thrift Store?

As one who doesn't leave, I am privy to many sad tales of disillusionment from those who could not find jobs here, or stores selling their favorite cosmetics, or a little Conch house to rent for under $1,500 a month.

A year or two down the road I am sure to hear from those same former Key West citizens, feeling nostalgic for the islands. They phone at odd hours, requesting updates on the activities of old lovers, friends and bosses. They tell me about their air-conditioned jobs, fat salaries and benefits and their spacious homes. Then they ask if they can crash at my house for two weeks next winter.

Back in the mid-1980s I worked at City Hall in the office of Mayor Richard Heyman. The mayor received an unbeliev-able number of letters from people who'd heard of Key West and wanted information on how they might find jobs and homes here. Usually we sent the classified section of the local paper and that would be the end of the matter. One enterpris-ing guy offered to donate a kidney for the guarantee of a life-time job and home in Key West.

When I waitressed on Duval Street I remember serving couples so sad little gray clouds were clearly visible over their heads.

"Tomorrow we go back home." they would explain. "But we're going to try to find a way to move down here perma-nently."

"What do you do?" I would ask.

"We're nuclear physicists," the answer might be.

"Ever waited on tables?"

Big laughs.

"I'll cry all winter missing Key West," Thea told my husband Michael the other day.

"Why don't you stay then?" he asked.

"How would I live?" Thea asked. "Teachers salaries here are half what they are at home."

"Yeah, but here we get paid in sunshine, and flowers and perfect weather," Michael said.

Last night as the nearly full moon rose, Michael and I went for a walk. We came upon a profoundly fragrant jasmine bush, so sweet my knees buckled. Michael picked a tiny blossom from the bush and held it to my nose, while I inhaled dramatically.

"Enjoy it, baby," he said. "That's this week's pay, plus your Labor Day bonus."

Eileen Bridges

The King's Southernmost Fan Club, the Snorkeling Elvises.
The 100% polyester, practically indestructible Elvis jumpsuit
is suitable for snorkeling, partying, parading, or changing
the oil in your pick-up truck.

A Little Bit of Elvis

Elvis impersonator Otis May, founder of the king's south-ernmost fan club, says he now knows why Elvis Presley wore sunglasses at night.

"People are snapping your picture all the time when you're Elvis," May says. "Flashes are constantly going off in your face."

"We must have been photographed at least 300 times last night," Valerie May says. "And downtown was actually pretty dead last night."

The Mays call the phenomenon "the Elvis thing."

It all began a few years ago when the Mays dressed up as Elvis and Priscilla for Fantasy Fest. Before the Elvis thing, thanks to Otis' costume dealer cousin in Memphis and their own inventiveness, the Mays had won lots of prizes for their fantastic costumes. But nothing in their masquerading past had prepared them for the amazing and unabashed adulation heaped upon them when they took to the streets as the king of rock 'n roll and his dark-eyed queen.

"People want to touch you. To give you money. To carry

your guitar case," says Otis May. "You've never felt anything like it."

Today in Key West, there are around 13 Elvis impersonators and roughly the same number of Priscillas. They call themselves the Snorkeling Elvises, inspired by the Parachuting Elvises portrayed in the movie *Honeymoon in Vegas*. The Snorkeling Elvises Fan Club is one of 250 officially sanctioned by Graceland. Their local charity (all Elvis fan clubs must have one) is the Monroe County Association of Retarded Citizens.

In addition to sponsoring an annual Blue Hawaii Beach Party fundraiser for the MARC group home, the Snorkeling Elvises appear frequently at local events. They arrive in a pink Cadillac.

Sometimes a group of Elvises in white, gold-studded jumpsuits don scuba equipment and descend 25 feet to participate in the annual Underwater Music Festival at the Looe Key National Marine Sanctuary. Photographs of the Snorkeling Elvises appear in newspapers all over the world.

The official Snorkeling Elvis jumpsuit costs $250, but it's practically indestructible, and includes the Elvis wig and sideburns. The suit is polyester which means it's hot. Yes, you sweat a lot, but it's also wash-and-wear.

"You can wear it snorkeling, partying, in long parades, and even to change the oil in your pickup truck," Otis May says.

Priscilla's costume calls for a $50 foot-high beehive wig, lots of '60s era eye make-up, a pastel mini-dress and high heels.

"Every Priscilla's hair has to be the way Elvis wanted it to be," Valerie May explains. "Elvis designed her hairstyle and her black eye-liner. She had to wear that eye-liner at all times - even when she went into the hospital to give birth to Lisa."

The Mays visit Otis' hometown of Memphis every August 17, the anniversary of Elvis's death. They pay homage to the

King's memory at Graceland where they mix and meet with thousands of fellow Elvis fans who spend that day there, too, to remember and compare lives.

"When I tell people I'm originally from Memphis, they say 'You mean you lived this close to Graceland and you moved away?' They just can't believe any Elvis fan would chose to leave Memphis," Otis says.

Every Fantasy Fest a bigger crowd of Otis May's old Memphis pals buy Elvis costumes from his cousin, and come down to Key West to be Snorkeling Elvises.

"Sometimes they're a little reluctant to try it," Otis May explains. "But the new Elvises always tell us it's the most fun they've ever had."

Same for the Priscillas, says Key West real estate agent Debra Benedict, an ardent Priscilla impersonator.

"Of course we Priscillas are just satellites. The Elvises are the big thing," Benedict says. "But until you put on that Priscilla wig you cannot even begin to imagine how incredible the Elvis thing is! Even as a Priscilla, you become part of something much bigger than yourself."

"What makes the Elvis thing so great is that you instantly become a celebrity. You can know what it's really like," explains is May. "You put the costume on and instantly, you're a huge star. Take the costume off and you're you again."

"We're careful not to over-expose this thing," he says. 'We only need to do it once in a while - 'cause a little bit of Elvis a long, long way."

Mike Perez

A fresh generation of Conchs, growing up on the water
just like their fathers, and their father's fathers. Danny Mira,
Mikey Perez, and Arlo Haskell.

The Great Escape

L ast Thursday night my son Mikey enthusiastically told me of his weekend plans.

"A bunch of us are sleeping out on an island tomórrow night," he said.

"Oh Mikey," I cried, as my heart clutched, "Do you really have to do that again?"

"Yes, Mom," he said. "See, it's a survival thing. We boat out and get dropped off on this deserted island before the sun goes down. No bathrooms. No water. No food. We cut open coconuts and drink the milk. We catch fish with our bare hands. If we don't catch any fish we have to kill rats, roast them the fire, and eat them.

"It's just like *The Lord of the Flies* out there," Mikey teased, adding fuel to the bonfire of my anxieties. "You know - survival of the fittest."

It actually took me a while to realize that he was kidding. Still, I don't like the idea of a bunch of unsupervised teenagers setting up camp far from civilization, and Mikey knows that all too well.

"Please be careful," I implored "Anything could happen out there! You could get hurt! What if you need stitches? What if you have an appendicitis attack."

"Mom, you're talking nonsense," Mikey sighed. And he was probably right. So I gave up, put my scary visions away, and went on without giving Mikey's camp-out another thought until bedtime Friday. Just before I turned out the light, I watched the news. The weather forecast for the Keys? High winds and rain.

I didn't sleep much that night, imagining Mikey and his pals on their barren island. What if they roasted marshmallows? Once at Girl Scout camp I watched as a girl was accidentally poked in the eye by her best friend's sharp marshmallow roasting stick. I remembered her being carried, kicking and screaming, to the counselor's car for the ride to the hospital.

Around 1 a.m. fat raindrops began clattering noisily on my tin Conch house roof. The wind began to blow hard and toss the tree boughs and plants on the deck outside my window. I imagined Mikey and his friends, huddled in flimsy sleeping bags, shivering, wet and hungry as the northern winds chilled the campsite, and a torrential rainfall doused their fire.

Poor brave Mikey! How he would suffer! And of course the campers had no choice but to await the dawn when they could jump into their boats and head for their homes. But what if pirates came along in the middle of the night and stole the boats? How would they get home then?

Just before dawn I finally fell into a thin, bad-dream laced sleep. At 8 a.m. I phoned Mikey's father on Cudjoe Key.

"They're back on shore," Mikey's father told me. "Now they're eating pancakes over at Venture Out."

Ahhh. At last I slept.

On Monday, which was Mikey's 16th birthday, he happily

told me about the camp-out. "Oh Mom," he said happily, "we watched the sun come up and it was amazing. A couple of birds flew past the sunrise. There was a sailboat silhouetted on the horizon. It was so awesome! "

'Wasn't it raining?" I asked. 'Weren't you wet?"

"It wasn't raining at sunrise," Mikey said. "I think maybe it rained a little at night. But we were in our tents. We were cozy and warm."

"Did you stay up all night?" I asked anxiously.

"No," Mikey said. 'We actually went to bed pretty early. By twelve. "

"You know Mom," Mikey said, "there's nothing like communing with nature. There's nothing like getting away from it all.

"Maybe next time you camp out I'll go along, too, Mikey. I'd like to get away from it all."

"No. You can't come Mom," Mikey said.

"Why not?" I asked.

"Because, Mom," Mikey said. "You're a part of it all."

Posing with Captain Tony, a guy always ready for a photo.

"Our lives change like weather, but a Legend never dies."
– *Jimmy Buffet, "Last Mango in Paris"*

Last Mango in Paris

What do you call him, I wondered, as we knocked on his door. He's been Captain Tony since he arrived on the island the 1950s and captained a charter-boat. He owned and operated Captain Tony's Saloon, where, he recalls, he once watched literary lords Tennessee Williams and Truman Capote ballroom dancing together "like a couple of grandmothers." He was mayor of Key West during of the island city's most golden glory days. *The New York Times* dubbed him the "Salt of Key West."

He even come back from the dead. A few years ago, he suffered a heart attack, and was whisked away from the local hospital in the middle of the night to be ambulanced to Miami for heart surgery. The following morning, when his fellow patients saw his bed and his room empty, they speculated that Captain Tony had not made it through the night. A rumor that he had died swept across the island like a wildfire. But two weeks later he was back in town, with a repaired heart and a new episode to laugh about - his own death.

Captain Tony's life story has been adapted to the big screen in Hollywood. There is a sizzling biography in the works.

A pretty young woman answered the Captain's door. Between hugs, handshakes and introductions, I felt like a little kid, with a big, happy grin on my face. For minutes I was speechless. The 80-year-old captain beamed as he rose from his chair to greet his guests. He moved an ashtray from the table to the floor, explaining, "I have one bad habit only: I smoke."

He introduced his wife Marty, the lady who answered the door. She is a third her husband's age, pretty and prim as a schoolteacher. Several kids appeared, the youngest of the 13 he has fathered in his life. ("So far . . ." he likes to joke.) The little boy and teenage girl eased gracefully into the background as their famous father held court at the kitchen table.

There were scrapbooks piled high on the table. I'd come to borrow some photographs. But before we got down to business, Captain Tony schmoozed a bit. He told us how great we looked, and teased my husband Michael about coping so gracefully with the challenge of living with me, "a member of the opposite sex."

"Remember the time when everybody thought you'd died from the heart attack?" I asked him.

"Yes," he says, smiling. "A lot of people in Key West still think I'm dead."

A couple of weeks ago, when the Planet Hollywood chain opened a restaurant in Key West amid great publicity and a big, invitations-only bash, featuring movie stars and local celebrities, Captain Tony was not on the guest list.

"I probably wouldn't have gone anyway," he grinned ruefully. "I don't like crowds much, and if I'm not the center of attention, I don't really want to be there."

He smiled as he said it, but it was clear he'd been hurt by

the slight. It's not that he minds missing another party. He's partied enough for two more lifetimes. It's just that he's done so much for Key West's image. He's a living legend, the guy Jimmy Buffett wrote about in the song, "Last Mango In Paris." Jimmy even used to fly Captain Tony to his concerts, seat him in the audience, and introduce him to the ParrotHeads just before he sang Last Mango.

How could Planet Hollywood not know that having a party Key West and not inviting Captain Tony is like having a mass and not inviting the priest?

When we got to the scrapbooks, we paused frequently to look and listen while Tony told the stories that went with the pictures. They were good stories of old Key West.

There was an aged photo of Tony and two daughters posing with a 1400-pound tiger shark on Garrison Bight. The teeth from that same shark, Tony told us, are now on exhibit at the Smithsonian Institution. There's a picture of Tony in a tuxedo, smoking a cigarette in the doorway of Captain Tony's Saloon, as he awaits arrival of his daughter Coral on her wedding day. Photos of the Captain in the *Wall Street Journal. The New York Times. The Miami Herald. People Magazine.*

The stories kept coming. Marty fixed coffee. The beautiful daughter wandered into the kitchen for some lunch.

"I'd like to find a nice young man for my daughter there," Captain Tony said, his famous baggy blue eyes twinkling. "If he'll give me a pig and two sheep, he can have her."

Susan Pitts

A favorite annual Christmas display in Paradise:
Santa in a hammock in the yard of the
Mermaid and the Alligator Guest House.

A Week of Hell In Paradise

I got a love letter from my husband Michael the other night. It was waiting for me on the kitchen table when I arrived home from work. I didn't read it right away. I saved it until after I had taken a long hot shower, shampooed the cigarette smoke out of my hair and dug the parmesan cheese and marinara sauce out from under my fingernails. As the clock struck 1 a.m., I brewed a pot of chamomile tea and curled up on the couch to read his message.

The first time through, I read it fast; the next time, slow; the third time, even slower, admiring Michael's handwriting and the sweet way he has of turning a phrase. Each time through, I savored the "I love you" and "I miss you" at the bottom of the page. Finally, I turned out the lights, climbed into bed, wrapped my arms around my sleeping husband, and whispered, "I love you, and I miss you, too." He didn't budge.

The next afternoon, before I left the house for work, and another dizzying round of waiting on tables, I wrote Michael a nice long letter. I told him how much I missed sharing meals with him, and how much I was looking forward to spending time with him again. I left his letter on the kitchen table, where I knew he'd find it a few hours later.

Pretty crazy, huh? Here we are living together in paradise, and we can't find 10 minutes to spend together. It's like this every year at this time. Christmas week, or Hell Week, as some of us in the service industry call it, is the most difficult week of the year. It's nobody's fault. There's no one to blame. It's a simple matter of logistics. How can one tiny island, and 25,000 full-time residents, cope with the needs of thousands of hungry, thirsty, curious and fun-seeking holiday tourists? Sometimes it seems impossible. Maybe it is impossible, yet each year on Christmas Day, and every day of the week that follows, visitors pour into town, crawling along U.S. 1, in bumper to bumper traffic, heading for downtown Key West and parking places that can take several hours to find. The same sort of thing, perhaps not quite so frenzied, seems to happen in March, when northerners find themselves unable to face one more day of wintery gloom and flood into sunnier places like our islands.

Michael is a tour guide. He drives a trolley, a particularly treacherous task at this time of the year. He rises before dawn, leaves the house before eight, and returns home after dark, exhausted and often too tired even to eat. At this time of the year we might go for days without seeing each other, communicating with midnight letters and hurried phone calls.

I leave for work around 4 p.m., wait tables till 11:30 or so, and stagger home around midnight. As any waiter knows, it is impossible to hop into bed and fall directly asleep after an 8-hour shift of waiting tables. It takes a while to wind down. Sleep seldom comes easily, and when it does, it is often filled with weird dreams of endless rows of tables full of angry customers demanding salads and beers and more garlic bread and extra sauce.

"Are you always this busy?" astonished customers sometimes ask, as they wait for their dinners and watch the crowds of anxious customers lining up at the door of the restaurant. Sometimes the anxiety builds, tempers flair, and sadly, adults begin to resemble their cranky children. They become whiny, irritable, inconsolable.

"Maybe you're too busy to take care of us," one grouchy diner snarled at me when I didn't take his wine order as quickly as he thought I should. "Maybe we should dine elsewhere tonight."

Yeah, I thought to myself, stung by his harsh tone and suddenly fighting back a week's worth of frustrated tears. How about Cleveland?

Owen Wagner was an actor and a historian, so he really loved posing as Henry Flagler, the guy who built the Overseas Railroad. The railroad connected Miami to Key West. It ran from 1912 until the great hurricane of 1935, when it was destroyed. Later it became a highway. Here, Owen (right) poses with local historian Earl Adams, in an historical re-enactment.

The Big O

The Big O would have loved his send-off, everyone agreed. His name was Owen Wagner. He was a trolley driver and he was 67 years old. He was considerably older than his fellow workers but they all loved him, each of them for their own reasons, and all of them for his brilliant sense of the absurd. He could always make them laugh.

He died in the summertime. One evening a few weeks later, just before sunset, a group of Owen's friends and co-workers gathered in Gerry Frantz's Duval Street apartment to hoist a few in memory of the Big O. Owen Wagner was there, too, in the form of six pounds of ashes in a box on the dining room table.

Owen made his living driving up and down Key West's most famous thoroughfare. At night, he often met his friends there. He loved Duval Street. Just before he died, he asked that his ashes be spread along the mile-long street that stretches from the Gulf of Mexico to the Atlantic Ocean.

"He's going to be spread from coast to coast," said Greg

Jones, a trolley driver who was Wagner's roommate.

"He never made a hit on Broadway, but he's making a hit on Duval Street tonight," said driver Rex Maynard.

As darkness fell over Key West, the group boarded a trolley. Jones handed out plastic cups filled with the Big O's ashes. As driver Raoul Emanuel guided the trolley slowly through the thick Friday night traffic, they tossed the ashes, cup by cup, to the street below.

"What are you throwing off of there?" asked the driver of a jeep, stopped behind the trolley at a light.

"An old trolley driver," replied Jones.

Owen Wagner taught high school English and history in Beaver Falls, Pa. before retiring in Key West. As the Old Town Trolley's unofficial historian, he spent many hours in the library researching the various dates, facts and fables that make up the script of the trolley tour.

But Owen will be remembered best for his humor. Back in Pennsylvania he worked weekends as a stand-up comic. He did outlandish impersonations of Walter Cronkite and W.C. Fields. Owen was quick with a quip, and very wise.

"He was the oldest and the hardest working driver," said ticket agent Cathy Munoz.

Wagner liked to pull his packed trolley up front of Cathy's ticket booth and say "Ladies and gentleman, say hello to my seventh wife." Then he'd yell to her "Did you find that 50 dollar bill I left under your pillow this morning, honey?"

Cathy helped Wagner arrange for in-home services from Hospice of the Florida Keys when his condition worsened several weeks before he died of pneumonia.

One day, shortly after Wagner took to his bed for the last time, Cathy was at his home, as she often was during Owen's last days. They were laughing it up, as usual.

"Well," Cathy said, glancing around her friend's modest room. "I guess this is all going to mine soon."

On the day before he died, Owen was so sick, his suffering so terrible, that Cathy broke down and cried. Owen watched her silently for a few seconds. Then he picked his head up off the pillow and said to her, "Hey — what are you crying about, honey? This is all going to be yours soon!"

"It was just like him to make me laugh when I was feeling so bad," Cathy says.

My husband Michael, a trolley driver, and I, were along on the Big O's last ride up Duval Street. And although it happened eight years ago, the Big O is still a part of our lives. He shows up in conversations from time to time, and when he does, we remember that night we tossed his ashes.

"I'll never forget him," Michael says. "I've thought about him a hundred times driving on Duval Street. As long as you live in someone's memory, you don't die."

Mike Perez, Sr.

*Graduation Day! My son Miguel, celebrating college graduation
with his parents, (left to right): Michael, his stepfather, Mike,
his father, me, his mom, and assorted girlfriends.*

His Key West

For a long time I was in the cozy habit of a daily telephone chat with my old friend Mike Perez. Every afternoon I'd call him. Or he'd call me. Ostensibly our conversations were about our son, who is 17 years old now, the result of our short, long ago marriage.

But Mike and I always found lots more than our boy to talk about. We talked about what was going on in his family. In mine. The weather. Controversies. Jokes. Deaths. Marriages. How much Key West has changed.

Mike had the keys to my house. I to his. When he was away we'd feed his dog. When we were away he checked on our place.

Through the years Mike has fixed plenty of things at our house - silly things that most people can handle without professional help. As he installs a curtain rod, or tightens a door handle he mutters and shakes his head.

"Intellectuals," he says.

And yet, I've sometimes repaid his favors with music.

During the course of our relationship he's developed a taste for Beethoven, particularly piano and violin sonatas.

A few months ago my husband and I drove to Miami with our son and Mike. Mike, who's always been one of those guys who has trouble sitting still, drove our car while we sat in the back seat. All the way to Miami he entertained us with funny stories of growing up in Key West.

When he was a little boy, Mike said, the DDT trucks regularly rolled through neighborhoods, releasing dense clouds of mosquito poison. The children would gather together and follow the slow-moving truck, gleefully dancing in the weird smoke of DDT fumes. If he and his cousins misbehaved, their grandmother Norma would warn, "You kids better be good or you won't be allowed to play in the DDT."

And that, Mike said, was an unbearable thought. The DDT truck was a thrilling high point in their lives.

When I told him I was worried about whether or not our son would be able to get into the college of his choice with a barely B average, and unremarkable SAT scores, Mike told me not to worry.

"I went to school with a lot of guys a lot dumber than our kid," Mike assured me. "And they graduated from Key West High and went away to college and got degrees. They're big shots today."

Six months ago, one of those educated big shots Mike grew up with offered him a job developing land in Central Florida. On New Year's Day, Mike told me he'd decided to leave Key West. A month ago he finally did.

"He's a Conch," his mother said to me. "He can't stay from Key West for long. He'll be back."

But I'm not so sure. His departure felt very real to me. And in many ways, it made a lot of sense. His Key West, the island he introduced to me 20 years ago, with its unpainted buildings grown silver in the sun, all-night parties on Smathers

Beach, and sweet, dumb innocence, is gone. The son we raised is grown and ready to fly.

A few days after his father left, my son pulled out an old photo album of his baby and early childhood days. Many of the photos feature Mike and me. Young. Proud. Happy.

"Does it make you sad to look at these old pictures of you and my dad?" my son asked.

I thought about my answer for a long time.

"Not at all," I told him. "Those were great times. Having a baby was a lot of fun."

"I guess this is it," Mike Perez said, mocking drama on the day he left Key West. "I guess it's finally over between us."

"Oh no," I said, dramatizing back at him. "It's not over between us. And it never will be!"

"I guess I can't shake her!" he shrugged, as he shook my husband's hand goodbye.

Contributed

My friend, the prodigy: Eugenie, in 1966. We were only 16 then!
With her music she gave me tantalizing glimpses of the world
beyond the little country town where I lived and she weekended.
Back then, she was the most dazzling, sophisticated girl I knew.

Roll Over Beethoven

R ecently my good buddy Carolyn told me she'd read
that rats listening to Mozart found their way through a
maze faster than those listening to something else.
What else? Snoop Doggie Dog? Wynonna Judd? John Philip
Sousa?

"What happens to rats listening to the Schubert?" I asked.
'The article only mentioned Mozart," Carolyn said.

I like listening to the Trout Quintet when I write, envision-
ing myself a happy fish, swimming easily through the difficult
waters of composition, buoyed by moody Schubert's rippling
phrases.

Still, I considered Carolyn's Mozart news. The job of writing is not, after all, very different from being a hungry rodent
fighting its way through a confounding maze. Could Mozart
help me find my way? It was worth a try. I plugged Mozart 's
"Requiem" into my player... and completed the first 33 pages
of a novel I have long dreamed of writing.

Just kidding.

A while ago I discovered that I could quite easily locate long lost friends via my computer and the World Wide Web. One of these was a pianist named Eugenie. When we were kids, Genie's family had a weekend home near mine in upstate New York. During the week she stayed in New York City and went to school there. Weekends she came to the country where her somewhat Bohemian parents maintained another home. I was often invited to her culturally lavish house to hang out. She was dazzling, small and beautiful; the most sophisticated girl I knew.

Genie practiced on a baby grand piano, improbably jammed into a tiny study off the living room. She played for hours every day. Even on weekends. I loved watching her tiny hands blurring over the keys. It was impossible to read (books were my refuge then) while Genie played. I could only listen in awe. She played a lot of Chopin that season of our friend-ship, and the experience began my lifelong devotion to Chopin's dreamy music.

We fooled around a lot, too. Genie played a full-blown ver-sion of "The Star Spangled Banner" while I bellowed the words in baseball stadium soprano. I played the flute. She taught me songs like "Smile" and "Satin Doll" and the theme from "The Umbrellas of Cherbourg." We practiced a Handel flute and piano sonata to perfection. I still have the music, with Genie's pencil markings vaguely evident on it, to this day.

When Genie got a driver's license, we spent Sunday after-noons driving about the countryside in her parents' Volkswagen, smoking cigarettes and talking about boys. She told me about her boyfriend Tad, who put hot jazz on the turntable when they necked.

"He knows it drives me crazy," she said, smiling mysteriously.

We grew up and lost touch.

Through the years I imagined my old friend Eugenie as a great diva, playing concerts on every continent. One day I found that her college listed its alumnae on the Internet. I found her address. I could have written. But I was too excited for a delay. I phoned. Genie answered.

She teaches music at an Ivy League college. She's married to Tad. They have two grown daughters. She did not remember me.

"We played the theme from 'The Umbrellas of Cherbourg,' I said. "You cried when you told me about the movie."

"I cried?" she said, perplexed.

"We were sixteen," I said. "You dyed my hair red and I sang the 'Star Spangled Banner' like Kate Smith."

"I dyed a lot of girls' hair red in those days," she laughed.

"You drove a VW and you made me love Chopin," I said weakly.

"Chopin?" she said, as if she'd never heard of him. "But my favorite composer has always been Mozart."

Sabrina Maxwell

*An old photo of me in the summer of 1976, wearing my
Jimmy Carter for President T-shirt, taking a break on the
Appalachian Trail. Twenty years later I had the opportunity
of showing this photo to President Carter. He loved it!
And autographed it for me.*

Spirit of '76

After only one week as a museum help temporary, I qualified as a staff member at Truman Little White House, and as such was invited to be at the museum, along with the other employees, to meet President and Mrs. Jimmy Carter as they arrived for a dinner party on New Year's Eve. At first I couldn't decide whether or not I wanted to stand outside the Little White House just after dusk to greet the Carters. For one thing I didn't feel like a true staff member, and for another, I was afraid of being seized with celebrity stage fright.

But whenever I mentioned to anyone that I might meet President and Mrs. Carter, they were intrigued. Everyone I know calls Jimmy Carter their favorite president. And so I decided that I owed it to my friends, and my future grandchildren, to go.

In an old photo album I found a picture of myself taken in the summer of 1976, right before I moved to Key West. In it I am wearing a Jimmy Carter for President T-shirt, taking a break from a hike on the Appalachian Trail. It was the summer of the Tall Ships in New York, and the U.S. Bicentennial. It was a time of high spirits and great hope. Everywhere you went, everybody was crazy for Jimmy Carter.

In a raucous Key West bar, a few months later, I watched the amazing election returns on television as America made the sunny man from Plains, Georgia its 39th president.

I had my little picture blown up to page size, and carried a pen with me to the Little White House on New Year's Eve. Having a mission, I figured, would save me from being nervous, and it did. But it didn't save me from being thoroughly awestruck when I met President Carter and the gentle Rosalynn.

The Carters moved with lightening speed through the short line of Little White House employees. The President approached each of us with his hand extended, ready for shaking, a benevolent smile on his face. He's the kind of man who makes you feel warm and special, all in an instant. And he exudes an unmistakable glow of greatness.

"It's a great pleasure to meet you, President Carter," I said brightly.

"We're honored to have you here, Mrs. Carter," I said to Rosalynn. "Welcome."

And then, they were gone. That's when I remembered my picture and my mission. I found a handsome teenager in the Carter party and showed my picture to him. The kid, who exhibited a junior version of the President's magnanimity, was Chip Carter.

"My grandfather would love to see this," Chip said. So I busted out of formation, and ran up ahead to the other end of the receiving line. Meanwhile, Chip approached the President and said, "Grandpa, a lady here has a neat picture to show you."

The President turned around and looked as I held up my

picture.

"It's me, in 1976, on the Appalachian Trail," I blurted quickly. "See! I'm wearing a Jimmy Carter for President shirt. Do you see your face here?"

"I love this picture," he said, beaming.

'Would you like to sign it?" I asked.

"I would be honored," he said, and without hesitation, using his right leg as an impromptu desk top, he quickly signed my photo.

And then, it really was over.

I can't remember what the Carters wore, or how their faces looked. What remains in my mind is the memory of a sensation of belovedness, the Carter's embodiment of hope - and that unmistakable glow of greatness.

In the early '80s Peter Hughes and I stood at the gates of the chic
Gingerbread Square Gallery at 907 Duval Street, for seasonal shows
by local artists. The gallery was owned by Mayor Richard Heyman.
Peter called us hostessettes and phoned me before shows to arrange
for our clothes to compliment and coordinate. Here we are, in 1984,
welcoming Stell Adams, and her constant companion "Sugar".
Stell, a painter and a psychic, was a cousin of Tennessee Williams,
who also aspired to be a great painter and showed his works at
the Gingerbread Square Gallery. At a show of works by the great Van
Eno, the artist was thin, hollow-eyed and weak. Peter told me Van was
dying of AIDS, which was very new at that time. Peter called it the
"disease du jour." Then Peter said he'd just bought himself a health
insurance policy, just in case he developed AIDS. "It could happen,"
Peter said grimly. Within the decade, it did.

Hummingbird On a Moonbeam

This week's magnificent full moon was so bright it hurt your eyes. A year ago, when March's full moon rose, Peter Hughes died, just as he planned to, a few minutes after sunset, as the first slanting rays of the rising moon beamed into his room.

Peter died in a tiny Conch house on Georgia Street, while March winds blew and spring breakers yelled and splashed noisily in a pool somewhere on the other side of a fence in Peter's back yard.

The summer before, my husband Michael, son Mikey and I had attended a pool party with Peter. He was thin and pale even back then. His beautiful golden hair, ravaged by illness and chemotherapy, was in sparse gray tufts. He went into the pool briefly, somehow found the energy to play with Mikey, then came out and sat on a beach wrapped in a towel. In spite of the terrible July heat, he was feverish and chilled at the same time.

"If you grow up and you get cancer and they tell you that you need to have chemotherapy," Peter said to Mikey, "don't do it!"

Growing up was not something Peter ever wanted to do. Being an interior designer in Key West, when his talents earned him a fraction of what they would have in his native Philadelphia, was Peter's way of maintaining his free spirit. He never plugged into the establishment; always loved the spontaneous and the avant-garde. His tastes were never trendy. He was stylish, but offhandedly so.

Peter was an uncomplicated man emotionally, too. When he was sad, he drooped visibly and was not too shy to ask for a hug. When he was happy, his joy was expansive and contagious.

His manners were Philadelphia perfect, but he was no snob. One of Peter's endearing charms was his habit of nicknaming people. I was forever "Ms. P" even after I married Michael Keith, because when met my last name was Perez. Richard Heyman, owner of the Gingerbread Square Gallery, was "Uncle Dick." Writer Sharon Wells was "Wellsy." Karen Rosenblatt was "Rosa."

A gray sky could turn Peter's mood dark faster than anything. He worshipped the sun, loved the beach and the sea.

Peter was creative director at the Gingerbread Square Gallery. For 17 years he created the gallery window displays, each one fresh and remarkable. Six times the gallery moved, and each time Peter designed the new interiors.

He also remodeled Key West homes; some grand, some modest. He was particularly clever at managing space, a great talent on an island of almost miniature houses. His own homes, usually small, simple Conch houses, were masterpieces—eclectic and elegant.

Peter had rare gifts. Not only was he a brilliant idea man, but he was fully capable of executing his visions, without complaint, without hesitation. There seemed to be nothing Peter could not do with a little time and enough lumber, paint and fabric.

Somehow he made it all look so easy. Perhaps, once he was left alone, he sprouted wings like a hummingbird and was released from the laws of gravity. Maybe he really was magic.

Peter was sick for a long time, but last March the transition from terribly ill to dying happened very quickly - within a matter of days.

His passing was not easy. He was terrified of dying; he had made no peace with death. On the day he died, his friend John Kiraly calmed him for hours and talked to him about the impending full moon.

"When the full moon rises, you can ride into the universe on a moonbeam," John told Peter again and again that afternoon. "On a moonbeam."

Just after sunset, he did.

Happy times in the waiters' station at the Lighthouse Cafe.
My favorite busboy and adopted son, Nikki, (left) posing
with Jon Hynes, our brother in table service.

Nikki Vicki Brenda

When he lived in Key West we called him Nikki Vicki Brenda. And because his mother is a writer, like me, and because we once figured that I really could be his mother, age-wise, he called me Mom or Mama. For a few seasons we worked together at the Lighthouse Cafe. Nikki was a busboy and I was a waitress. We had fun pretending to the customers that Nikki was my son.

"Mom," he would say beseechingly, holding a tray aloft in one hand, the other akimbo, "when you dressed me like a girl when I was little, didn't you think it might mess my head up just a little?"

To a table of obviously gay guys, Nikki might chat for a few minutes and then, with a perfectly straight face, say, "Gentlemen, where are the wives tonight?"

Nikki knew by heart every word of the script of *Female Trouble*, the kooky John Waters film.

"I got a knife in my purse," he would hiss into my ear, as I tried to get an order from a table of grumpy tourists. "And I'm going to cut you up after work!"

It's a line from *Female Trouble*.

Nikki Vicki Brenda had not only a remarkable talent for comedy, but a magnificent voice, too. He mimicked Whitney Houston or Diana Ross perfectly. He danced. He whirled. He sang into a restaurant pepper mill as though it was a microphone. Then, just when his audience was truly mesmerized, he would stop, blush, and laugh self-consciously.

He told me that he'd tried to perform in a variety show in high school. But he'd lost his nerve, and rushed off the stage before he even got started. He sang in church when he was very young. He'd been an altar boy, too, in his hometown of Homestead, Florida.

In Key West, Nikki spent many hours volunteering at AIDS Help and Helpline. But he rarely mentioned his volunteer work. He rarely talked about anything serious. He was too busy making people laugh.

One of Nikki's two brothers was shot to death in Miami. The other is an officer in the Air Force, like his dad. His mother is a devout Christian. His parents have been divorced for a long time.

Nikki's family is loving, and supportive, but they have difficulty understanding his quirky genius. It's hard to watch someone with so much talent, so much intelligence, always fooling, ever the clown.

Eventually Nikki left Key West to live with his mother in Marianna, Florida. We exchanged letters. Nikki was a good writer, too. Insightful. Crazy. Hilarious. Heartbreaking.

"It's hard for me to get off the couch," he wrote a year after he left. "Things are going down the tubes for me healthwise."

It was the first time he'd mentioned to me that he was ill, though I knew.

"I have everything I could ask for here, but friends," he wrote. "Your letters make me so happy!"

I wrote a story about Nikki in the paper. I described what a great, funny, caring person he was, how much he'd given to Key West, how sick he'd become, and how hungry he was for mail.

After that Nikki was besieged with letters and cards from well-wishers, many of whom had never even met him. He was thrilled with the outpouring of compassion and his new pen pals, who kept him busy for the final six months of his life.

"Mama," he wrote in his last letter to me, "you know how much I love you! Still, one more hug can't hurt."

*Garth Bandell displays his show-stopping good looks in the
jungle paradise of his Key West back yard. Garth lives in
Virginia now, where he raises horses. In Key West he ran a
fabulous restaurant and an amazing aerobic dance class.*

Peep Show

A few weeks ago my son Mikey was home from school for Spring Break. On the first night he was here I went into his room to tuck him into bed. We were chatting softly when the late night quiet was shattered by the lonely midnight crow of a wild rooster.

"Oh Mama," he said happily, "I'm know I'm truly home when I hear that - the sound of my Key West."

The confused chickens of Old Town cockadoodledoo at all hours of the day and night. Further, they seem to have no sense whatsoever when it comes to getting to the other side of the street. Down here, we are accustomed to stopping our cars to let mama hens and their peeping chicks cross.

Visitors to the island seem enchanted by our flock of lost and unclaimed birdbrains. Many times at the Blue Heaven Restaurant I've seen tourists carefully photographing roosters as if they were some exotic tropical species. They feed them bits of bread and ask locals questions about where the chickens sleep and lay their eggs.

But not everyone is as charmed as our tourists and my Conch son by these runaway yardbirds. Many of our Old Town neighbors complain bitterly that the noisy roosters keep them awake too many nights. And I have a friend whose mother, brought up on a farm in Tennessee, wouldn't stay for lunch at Blue Heaven because she didn't want to eat in a yard with chickens scratching at her feet. No matter how good the food.

We love chicken. My husband Michael and I celebrate special events with fried chicken dinners at the Deli Restaurant. It's actually become a tradition for us. Any good news around here calls for Deli Restaurant fried chicken.

Michael phones ahead to the kitchen and says, to whoever answers, "Ask the cook to drop a couple orders of fried chickens for Michael, would you please? We'll be there in 20 minutes." He says it as if he knows all about the politics of the short order kitchen, when in fact, all he knows for sure is that fried chicken takes a while to fix. He likes to arrive at the Deli right when his chicken's coming out of the fat, find a seat, select two from the veggies of the day list, decide between a biscuit or corn muffin, and get down to business.

It's one of those Key West insider's secrets he's proud to know.

I remember the day my Nova Scotia uncle invited my cousins and me into the barnyard to watch him slaughter a chicken for our dinner. Since that day I have been intimately hip to the meaning of the term "like a chicken with its head cut off."

My friend Garth, who lives on a quiet as a Tennessee farm lane in Old Town, told me that his peace was recently disturbed when a rooster took up residence beneath the house next to his. The bird crowed from dusk till dawn keeping Garth and his neighbors awake night after night.

In desperation Garth posted a handmade sign on a telephone pole offering $100 reward to whoever could rid the lane of its raucous rooster.

The chicken posse arrived in the form of a mother, a father, and two young sons. The mother knocked on Garth's door and asked if the reward was still available. It was. With deep skepticism, Garth indicated to the family the location of rooster's hide-out beneath a neighbor's house.

The boys jumped out of the car with a chicken of their own. They placed it on the ground within view of the rene-gade rooster. Within seconds, Garth's lonely lane bird came out from under the house to investigate. With that the little boys scooped up the birds, one each, and jumped back into their car. The entire procedure had taken minutes.

Garth gave the mother the money and the family drove away with the fruit of the day's labors: chicken dinner and a hundred bucks.

Gail Brockway

*Happy scenes at the Lighthouse Cafe. The Lighthouse Cafe
is gone now, and so are the people who bought it and decided to
replace old staff with an all new one. Raymond (far left) and I were
good friends then. He got himself a bunch of nursing degrees and is
now employed at Sloan-Kettering Cancer Center in New York City.
He and Ron broke up a few years later, a shocking event at the start
of a whole cascade of changes in the fabric of Key West community.*

Ray Gets Fired

When my friend Ray phoned last night, I sensed a scary edge in his voice. I thought he might be calling to tell me that someone had died. I tensed, preparing for bad news.

"I just got fired," he said, his voice quivering. "I got fired - over the phone."

I met Ray six years ago when I worked as a service bartender at the Lighthouse Cafe. Ray was a waiter. He was quiet, sweet and sexy in a dark, smoldering sort of way I found irresistible.

"You remind me of the Italian boys I used to run with back home," I teased him. 'Whenever I get homesick for New York, I'll call you."

Ray has been working in restaurants since he was 15 and lied about his age to work in a fast-food hamburger joint in Cleveland, Ohio. He's always dreamed of becoming a nurse. But first he wanted to get his house finished, and save up the money to pay for nursing school.

After a year of bartending at the Lighthouse Cafe, I was promoted to the wait staff. Ray trained me and remained my mentor throughout my 5-year waitressing career.

Ray always worked hard. While most waitrons goofed off pretty regularly, he stayed in constant motion. He was a detail man, who made certain at the beginning of each shift that we had enough napkins folded and enough lemons cut. Sometimes his dedication was almost irritating. "You'd think he owned the place," we'd gripe. Actually, his devotion was vital. Someone had to care the way Raymond did.

On his twelfth anniversary with his lover Ron, Ray couldn't get the night off. So Ron came in for dinner. Alone. Ray waited on him. After I'd stopped at Ron's table to chat, an older lady at the next table asked, "Is that nice young man a friend of yours?"

"Yes," I answered. "He's celebrating his anniversary tonight."

Later, when he had a few minutes, Ray sat down to glass of champagne with Ron.

"It's too bad that man's wife couldn't be with him on their anniversary," the woman sighed. "Where is his wife?"

"Oh, that's his partner," I said, pointing to Ray. "They're not married exactly, but they've been sharing their lives for 12 years! Isn't it wonderful?"

The woman looked confused for an instant, as she sorted through the information. Then her face softened and she smiled.

"Yes, it is wonderful," she said.

Eventually, the Lighthouse Cafe was taken over by new owners, a couple who were new to Key West and island ways. Many longtime staff members split. But Ray, finally enrolled in nursing school, stayed. And so did I. Eventually we two were the only old-timers left. Then, a couple of weeks ago I quit. And last night, Ray was fired.

"We're going with an all new staff this season," he was told.

For a hardworking person like Ray to be fired from a job he's held for ten years is a terrible shock. My heart ached for him when he told me. I love Ray a lot, and I felt how bad he was hurting.

Of course Ray will be all right. He'll find another job to sustain him as he goes through nursing school. As employees go, he's a catch.

"You've seen a lot of changes over the years, haven't you?" people remark upon hearing I've been living here for 20 years.

Yes, I've seen changes. But the hardest changes aren't necessarily the ones you can see. Some of the scariest changes are the ones you feel. The face of Key West is changing, but so is the heart and the soul.

White Seal Bar, Miami, 1947. Henry "Basil" Gomez, (far right) got his nickname because of his resemblance to the actor Basil Rathbone. Before he became the Box Man he was a very dapper and popular young man about town. Here he is with Coast Guard buddies Rene Rojas, Mike Perez (in uniform), an unknown barmaid, and Van Gura.

Rene Rojas collection

The Box Man

When he died he was known in Key West as the Box Man because his only apparent possession or attachment was to a cardboard box that he carried with him wherever he went. He slept on the sidewalk, usually at the corner of White Street and Truman Avenue, wrapped in a black trench coat no matter what the weather, his head propped against his box.

That's how they found him one Tuesday night. Dead.

The Box Man appeared to be destitute, but he was not. A veteran's pension check was deposited into a bank account for him each month. From time to time he walked to the bank and withdrew cash to pay for the many cigarettes he loved to smoke. From various Cuban coffee shops on White Street he bought himself frequent Styrofoam cups of coffee. Sometimes people took pity on him and offered to buy his coffee, but he always refused their charity, assuring them he had money.

Nonetheless, he ate food forged from garbage in dumpsters behind Fausto's grocery and an apartment complex behind the Jehovah Witness Hall on White Street.

His real name was Henry Gomez. Key West friends called him Basil, after the actor Basil Rathbone. Like Rathbone, who played Sherlock Holmes in movies of the '30s, Gomez, the young man, was remarkably thin and gaunt. But he was movie-star dapper, too.

"He was one of the neatest men you have ever seen," remembers Mike Perez, a Conch who grew up with Gomez and knew him all of his life. "He was intelligent and clean. He always had a shoeshine and neat hair. He was very quiet and very nice. But there was a time bomb in him."

In 1943, during World War II, Mike Perez, Henry Gomez, and Rene Rojas enlisted in the Navy. They went through boot camp together, but were split up after that.

After the war, the same trio joined the Coast Guard in Key West for a two-year tour of duty. Perez and Rojas were buoy watchers. Gomez was assigned to a weather station in a light-house miles out at sea.

Perez recalls that Gomez stayed at the lighthouse for 90 days at a time. Then he came ashore for 30 days. Once, Gomez was somehow forgotten out at sea in his weather station, and remained there, stranded, for many days beyond the 90 scheduled ones.

"That's when he cracked," Perez says.

Basil Gomez recovered from his breakdown at the Veteran's Hospital in Coral Gables. Key Westers Mike Perez, brothers Kiki and Rene Rojas, and Danny Boza visited him there. Eventually Gomez went to a barber school in Miami. When he came back to Key West he worked for Sam Valdez's Gate Barber Shop.

In 1976, Mike Perez moved to Houston. When he returned, six years later, he was shocked to learn that the once elegant barber, Basil Gomez, was living in the streets, filthy and unkempt.

"Like Howard Hughes or somebody like that," Perez says.

So Basil Gomez's old friends, Perez, the Rojas's, Boza and Valdez, got together and agreed to chip in and get him an apartment.

"But it was no use," Perez recalls. "Basil didn't want our help. He liked living on the streets. Nobody knows why."

When Basil Gomez died last month, his sister requested that the VA give her an American flag to bury with him, to honor his service in World War II. And she got it. Mike Perez says he saw the flag at Gomez's small funeral.

"It's important for you to tell the story of Basil Gomez," Mike Perez told me. "People should know he wasn't a bum."

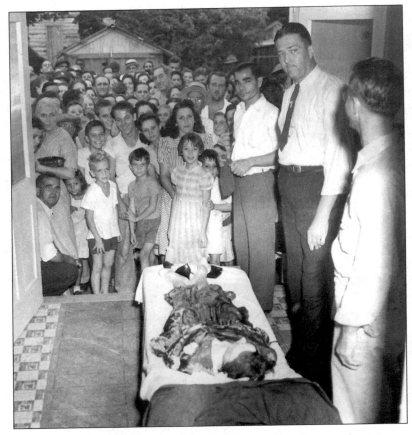

Miami Herald

The 7-years-dead body of Maria Elena Hoyos drew such an
audience (6,850 viewers in three days) that some entrepreneurial
Key Westers suggested that it be placed in a glass case and exhibited
as a tourist attraction. Her family wouldn't hear of it though,
and Maria Elena was re-buried in an unmarked grave
in the City Cemetery.

Weird Science

When songwriter Ben Harrison heard the story of creepy, crawly Count Carl von Cosel, Key West's infamous necrophiliac, and Maria Elena Hoyos, the object of his ghoulish ardor, he immediately felt his songwriting senses shift into overdrive.

Harrison began performing 'The Ballad of Maria Elena Hoyos" at his regular gig at the Bull and Whistle on Duval Street. Every time he did, his audience became enthralled by the weird rhapsody.

"Is that a true story?" people asked him incredulously.

"It is." Ben Harrison told them. "It really is. I promise."

Count von Cosel, who wasn't a count at all except in his mind, was an X-ray technologist at Key West's Marine Hospital. In the spring of 1930, the beautiful, but doomed beauty, Elena Hoyos, showed up at the hospital for blood tests and X-rays that revealed that she was suffering with advanced tuberculosis. Von Cosel was immediately smitten with 22-year-old Elena, whom he recognized from a dream he'd had forty years earlier.

Von Cosel determined to save Elena's life. With his own invention. It was a bizarre contraption that was connected by electrodes to the girl's wasting body. The treatments were hideously painful for Elena, but von Cosel's weird science was oddly reassuring, too. Her poor, heartbroken parents welcomed his devotion and ministrations. He kept up their hopes for their daughter's survival.

As Elena languished in her tiny bedroom, von Cosel brought her gifts of perfume, scarves, jewelry, and exotic fruits and candies. He bought her an elaborate mahogany bed, that barely fit through the door of the family's humble home. It was in that bed that Elena finally died, on October 25, 1931.

But she did not rest in peace. One moonless night, von Cosel unearthed her nearly fleshless bones and took them to his laboratory where he attempted to preserve what remained of Elena's sultry charms with regular soaks and washes. He fought an unending battle with insects, who continually found ways into Elena's nooks and crannies in spite of his painstaking precautions. The madman replaced Elena's rotting flesh with oiled silk, beeswax and balsam. He replaced her eyes with glass ones.

Eventually von Cosel's eerie project was discovered. It's difficult to keep a secret in Key West - especially one as odorous as necrophilia. Seven years after he'd kidnapped Elena, she was taken from him again.

Doctors autopsied Elena's remains, and reportedly found physical evidence of von Cosel's love. He was arrested.

Elena's body was exhibited in a local funeral parlor. Nearly 7,000 people came to see her. Teachers brought their classes. Reporters came from all over the country. Von Cosel's story caught the fancy of just about everyone in America.

One day the owner of a publishing company was in the

crowd at the Bull and Whistle when Ben Harrison sang/spoke the bizarre saga of von Cosel's undying love. The publisher asked Harrison if he would write a book about Maria Hoyos and Count von Cosel. He even offered to pay Harrison an advance to resurrect Key West's most twisted tale.

Harrison wrote the book, and since it appeared in local bookstores, it's been selling like crazy. Undying Love explores every mucky detail of the macabre legend and contains unbelievable quotes from von Cosel's own kooky narrative that appeared in *Scientific American* magazine.

Next time you've got a few hours to kill (you should pardon the expression) pick up Harrison's book. Halloween Eve might be a perfect evening for this gross and engrossing tale. You won't be disappointed.

Contributed

Katha Sheehan and a chicken friend watch the Gay Pride Parade from the door of the Chicken Store on Duval Street. Those guys in the parade are carrying the Rainbow Flag. Chickens and rainbows are basic to Key West living. We take both icons very seriously.

The Daily Scratch

In Key West we have whole shops about cats, several stores featuring all things Cuban, and now, a museum/shop devoted to those crazy little cluckers, and favorite symbol of Old Key West, the gypsy chickens. The Chicken Store salutes the tenacious spirit of the sturdy yardbird, and after a visit to the shop, you will, too.

There are plenty of people in Key West who can't imagine anyone admiring island chickens. What irks locals most, it seems, is the roosters' crow shattering the silence of the darkest hour of the night. While it is easy to sympathize with the hung over tourist who tries in vain to sleep with a gypsy rooster cockadoodledoo-ing outside his expensive hotel room window, it is difficult to understand how a local resident, with years of habituation under his belt, cannot tolerate the proud song of the remarkably resilient yardbird.

Our summertime neighbor, Thea, is in for a surprise when she arrives this week. Between the time that her winter tenants leave, and Thea arrives, we feed her summertime stray cats, Snake and Evander. Although the cats are well fed, they appear to have recently returned from Hell. Skinny. Scabby. Hungry. We recently discovered why. Just after their cat food dinner is placed before them on Thea's deck, neighborhood chickens show up and peck at the cats' tails as they are trying to eat. Soon the cats give up and surrender their bowls of food to the chickens, who eat their fill and then strut around the yard noisily clucking to the animal world that they have put one over the street cats once again. These are tough cats, mind you, battle scarred and mean-faced from many brutal encounters in dark, downtown alleys. But the chickens are tougher. And more persistent.

I related the story of our neighborhood's pushy chickens to my friend Katha Sheehan, whose idea it was to pay homage to our island's chickens by opening the Chicken Store.

"Did you know about that tail-pecking trick?" I asked her.

"Not that one," Katha said, "but I have heard about chickens doing just about anything and everything."

In our backyard habitat, the most active chicken of all is a runty little black hen, who hops about noisily, and enjoys perching like a hood ornament on top of trucks and cars. She poses and preens like a much prettier chicken and I have come to believe that there is a lesson for all of us in her haughty self-confidence.

Yesterday a gaggle of tourists gleefully shot photographs as a handsome, young Key West cop stopped his car, got out, and held up his hands to stop traffic at a busy Old Town intersection, to allow a mama chicken and her baby chicks to cross the street.

"This island is a bird sanctuary" a nearby pedestrian, observing the scene, explained to the charmed tourists. "It doesn't make any difference what species they are. All birds are protected here."

Whoever wrote the childhood story about the hen who ran

around the barnyard warning everyone she saw that the sky was falling, certainly understood the chicken personality. Very little deters a chicken from its mission, whatever that may be. Why did the chicken cross the road? Nobody knows. What we do know is that there is nothing chicken about a chicken. Undaunted they roam where they will, unintimadated by cars, tough cats, and toddlers tossing handfuls of pea rock, or teenagers on bicycles aiming to run them down.

For humans, surviving on this island grows ever more challenging. People are migrating to other habitats, where life isn't such a struggle. But I am habituated. I take my cue from the gypsy chickens. After many years of hand-to-mouth living, I find myself well adapted to the daily scratch.

The late Willoughby Sunshine Watherwax stars in one of America's best-selling posters, Fat Cat Capsizing.

Fat Cat Capsizing

Whenever I run into photographer Richard Watherwax, I ask him about his cat Willoughby - a fat feline with such a sunny disposition her middle name is "Sunshine." I met Willoughby on a visit to Richard's studio about five years ago, but she's been with Richard a lot longer than that. He adopted her from an animal shelter in New York City 16 years ago.

Willoughby spent her first few years as an apartment-bound city cat. Then Richard moved to Maine and opened a restaurant.

As a kitchen cat, Willoughby loved lapping up gravies, sauces and cream and nibbling bits of and fish. Sedentary by nature, she gained weight easily.

"We fed her like a queen," Richard says. "And she ate like a pig."

At her heaviest, Willoughby Sunshine Watherwax weighed 22 pounds.

"Some people are thin and some are fat," one vet

explained to Richard. "And so it is with cats."

Richard says Willoughby always loved the camera and the bright studio lights. Even as a kitten she was anxious to please. Early on Richard knew: Willoughby was a natural model.

Willoughby's greatest - though not only only claim to fame is a nationally distributed, bestselling poster called "Fat Cat Capsizing." In it, a series of 3 photographs illustrates the story of Willoughby falling backward off a bed.

Richard says he got the idea for "Fat Cat Capsizing" when he heard Johnny Carson make a joke about actress Shelley Winters capsizing in her bathtub.

"It was such a funny image," he says.

For a while Richard sold his posters, postcards and T-shirts - many of them featuring Willoughby - at the daily sunset celebration at Mallory Pier.

"Sometimes women would come up to me and ask me why I had allowed my cat to get so fat," Richard remembers. "They were not amused."

A while ago Richard decided to put Willoughby on a diet. But by that time Willoughby was a mature cat, set in her habits. She did not like eating smaller portions, and so Richard quickly gave up.

"The time of the diet marked the beginning of her downfall," Richard says.

In November, Willoughby was diagnosed with feline infectious peritonitis, a deadly virus. Richard took Willoughby for weekly visits to the vet on Stock Island. The vet regularly drained fluids from around her lungs and heart and prescribed a battery of medications. For a while she survived, one day at a time.

Last week Willoughby needed two trips to vet. Her weight had dropped to six pounds. Finally, Richard and her doctor agreed that it would be inhumane to keep her alive any longer.

On the day she died, Richard says he ran errands, ate breakfast out, balanced his checkbook and did anything he could think of to postpone the inevitable moment when he phoned the cab to take him and Willoughby on their last ride to the vet.

"I called ahead and told them exactly when I would be arriving," Richard said. "I walked into the vet's office, put Willoughby in her carrier on the counter, and I walked out. That was the last time I saw her."

As Richard told his story, tears shone in his eyes. I began to cry, too.

"I know," he said, sighing sadly. "You're crying because you're remembering all the pets you have loved and who have died."

Yes, I cried for them. But I also cried for all the people I have loved and who have died, and for all who are dying.

Richard Heyman, his partner, the great John Kiraly, and me,
on one of a thousand happy occasions. That's Kiraly's illustration
on the cover of this book.

Love Always

Four years ago this week Richard Heyman died. It rained when he died, and it's rained on this day every September since, which honors his memory. He loved rain as much as he loved sunshine and every other of nature's moods. He loved life.

Richard was twice elected mayor of Key West, and will probably go down in history as America's first gay mayor. But he was much more than that. I worked for Richard; and like everyone who did, I became a member of his extended family. Richard was a wise, compassionate and loving friend. Bigger than life. And now it seems, bigger than death, too.

The worst thing about missing someone who has died is heading for the phone to call them, and then remembering that they're no longer available to pick up at the other end of the line.

Old habits die hard. I head for the phone to call Richard less often than I used to, but I still do. And when I do there's that cold, sad thud in my heart, when I realize once again I can no longer tell him a joke and make him laugh his big, booming song of laughter.

He won't call me again, either, and sing that Stevie Wonder song, "I Just Called to Say I Love You," into my answering machine.

I think of Richard on the anniversary of his death, and on many other days as well. I once read that when someone you love passes on great love keeps them alive in your heart. I thought it was wishful thinking at the time, but today I know it's true.

I hear Richard's voice often. I'm not quite sure how. Is he a guardian angel perched on my shoulder, whispering into my ear? Or did I know and love him so well that I now know instinctively what he would say to me at each juncture?

Yesterday I awakened before dawn, with a fresh idea I felt I should get up and write. But it was raining, so I burrowed deeper under my quilt.

"Get going, June," the memory of Richard said. "Life is short."

On the day I found myself face to face with a woman who'd taken serious advantage of Richard's big heart and deep pockets, I felt myself bristle and search my brain for words, when I heard Richard's voice: "Let it go, June. I have."

And I did.

After trying to figure out what to do with Richard's collection of cards, letters, photographs, and souvenirs after he died, I understand the futility of trying to save a life by storing its parts like a puzzle in a box. I let stuff and things go now. Easily.

From Richard I am learning that life is not yesterday. Or tomorrow. Last year or next week. Life is always right now. And now. And now.

Join us on the worldwide web at:
www.JuneKeith.com

Ann L. Williams

One morning a blind chicken flew into my head, causing me
to drop two plates of banana pancakes into the dirt.
Customers laughed. The cook was furious. I thought to myself:
how did a nice girl like me end up in bacon and egg hell?
It was my last shift of waitressing.

Hell At Blue Heaven

Waitressing, they say, is like riding a bike. Once you learn how to do it, you don't ever forget. So, after a two-year sabbatical from waitressing, with Christmas shopping season fast approaching, I went in search of a position as a food and beverage server.

In spite of advice from wise, waiting friends who warned that the breakfast shift in any eatery is a sure route to bacon-and-egg Hell, when I was offered a job working the day shift at the famous Blue Heaven, I signed on. Breakfast from 8 a.m. till noon. Lunch till 3. All of it served outdoors in a garden beneath ancient hardwood trees.

Ricky's Blue Heaven Restaurant is located in a busy junction of earthy local color, at the corner of Thomas and Petronia streets in Bahama Village. The old neighborhood, with its friendly dogs, happy children, painted bicycles and nonstop action, is the kind of place that people without first-hand knowledge imagine all of Key West to be. Heartily praised in print by travel journalists and recommended regularly in travel guides, the Blue Heaven has become a must-see on every adventurous tourist's itinerary.

Blue Heaven customers are happy campers from the moment the host shows them to their painted table. Here is what they've been searching for! Atmosphere. Charm. Funky-looking island people. Cats. And live chickens.

"The cats don't bother the chickens?" customers ask.

"Who owns these chickens?" some want to know.

'Where do these chickens sleep?" a lady asks. 'Where do they lay their eggs?"

After a lengthy exchange that is a necessary part of every breakfast order - how do you want your eggs cooked? Potatoes or grits? Ham or bacon? Multi-grain or rye toast? Pancakes or banana bread? - there is little time for chicken chat. Little time for anything else at all except to fly into the kitchen, place the order, pray the cook is not too badly hung over, and dash back out again to refill empty coffee cups and run for more butter, or cream or syrup.

After my first eight-and-a-half-hour day of waitressing, just before I fell asleep around 8 p.m., my husband and I fondly recalled the bygone days of ninety-nine cent breakfasts at the Fourth of July Restaurant on White Street. Breakfast was Cuban toast slathered in butter, a slab of salty ham, grits and two eggs. The waitress never dreamed of asking how you wanted your eggs. Oh, you could request over-easy or scrambled or sunnyside up. But everybody's eggs came out the same. Fried. Who would argue over ninety-nine cent eggs?

Customers of the '90s warn, don't you dare break the yolks or I won't eat them. After a week of working at Blue Heaven, influenced by my fellow workers' blue nail polish, beads and dreadlocks, and their nonchalant approach to shaving, I began to feel the need for some body-piercing, or at least, an exotic tattoo. I described this longing to Cynthia, a trendy-looking kitchen worker, and the following day she brought me a batch of Skin and Ink magazines, from which I might find ways to fashion a trendier me.

My fellow servers at the Blue Heaven, clear-eyed beauties in Zen-decadent garb, are predominantly young. There is a reason for this. Only the very young can handle the breakfast shift with its inherent challenges and detail-laden script. A far-sighted baby boomer, with fading audio powers and a memory like Swiss cheese, is no match for the eggs-over-easy-or-else crowd.

And so, after three weeks and twelve breakfast shifts at the Blue Heaven, I bade farewell to my server sisters, Samantha, Renata, Vanessa, Melissa, and canceled my appointment with the tattoo artist.

Contributed

Johnny Conte. Many great women have loved him.
Many great women have lost him. He owns a restaurant in
Rockland, Maine, and is still unmarried. Linda is a happily
married brain surgeon in Miami.

The Other Woman
Is a Brain Surgeon

Thursdays I work at the Gingerbread Square Gallery. The gallery is cool and spacious, with soft gray walls. Classical music plays all day, and the paintings, tropical scenes with orchids, birds, jungles, beaches, starfish and staircases climbing into heavens, are like illustrations out of a fairy-tale book. People entering the gallery's subdued interior become immediately enchanted.

"If I can help you with anything," I say to lookers, just let me know."

I was halfway through my gallery greeting the other day when I suddenly stopped short and gasped. In the tiny crowd assembled at the door, I recognized a face I had hoped never to see again. Long ago I had stolen a man away from the woman who stood there gazing expectantly into the gallery.

She's still perfect, I thought, as I watched her and remembered a long-ago drama. Twenty years ago I was back in New York, hungry for a world that seemed ever beyond my reach.

High school and college were done. I was feeling aimless, unsettled.

Then I met Johnny, a brooding Italian who wooed me with fine dinners at elegant restaurants and long boozy evenings at places with names like Gertrude Hart's Golden Mirror Room. We talked endlessly. We laughed a lot.

Johnny drove a Cadillac, refused to wear jeans because everybody else did, and ran 10 miles a day before jogging was the thing to do. He'd lived in Europe. He'd been loved by foreign women. He'd sampled exotic cuisine. He'd been around.

After two years of dating Johnny, I wanted to be his wife. Johnny balked. If we didn't marry, I threatened, we were through.

But Johnny was not the marrying kind, he explained. He loved me. Wasn't that enough? No, it wasn't. So I said goodbye to Johnny. Secretly I was certain that in due time he'd miss me so much he'd come back to me and beg me to marry.

Instead, he met Linda. Linda wore tight denim waist jackets, and 5-inch platform shoes. She wore her blond hair long, a shimmering frame for a tiny, freckled face, as sunny and innocent as a daisy's. She was the coolest girl I'd ever seen. Smart, and chic, but nice, too - a model of all to which I aspired.

Linda drove a sports car. She took Johnny camping, rafting down rivers, and to her parents' posh home for dinner. Linda had already been married once. She'd once dated Jimi Hendrix. She was mad for Johnny, my rebel, and, to my utter horror, he was mad for her.

I flew to Florida, to nurse my broken heart on Ft. Lauderdale Beach. Winning Johnny back became the focus of my life. Every day for five months, I wrote long, crazy letters to Johnny. We spent hours on the phone.

"June," he said at last, "come home. I'll break it off with Linda if you'll come back to me."

There was no trace at all of Linda at Johnny's when I had finally wheedled my way back into his life. Missing also was my desire to be with him. After a few weeks, I left him for good.

Ten years or so ago I saw Johnny again. We had a good talk about the old days. He told me that Linda had graduated from medical school and was working at becoming a brain surgeon.

"Just my luck, I'll bash my head in some day, and Linda will be the doctor," I joked to Johnny. "She'll see it's me and perform a lobotomy."

But when I did see Linda again last Thursday, it didn't feel bad at all. She is a neurosurgeon now, with yacht-broker husband and a home in Miami. She's still friendly and personable. She gave me her phone number and asked me to call her next time I'm up there.

'This is such a beautiful gallery," Linda whispered reverently. "Is it yours?"

"Yes, it is," I lied. "I'm so glad you like it."

Gotham Studios, NYC

This photo hung on Frank Taylor's living room wall.
That's playwright Arthur Miller (top) sharing a ladder with producer
Frank (far left.) By the time this photo was taken, Frank told me,
Miller's marriage to Marilyn Monroe was over, and in spite of
the Hollywood smiles, no one else on the famous set was having
a very good time either. Arthur Miller and Frank Taylor
have died since this column originally appeared.

The Misfit

Key West publisher Frank Taylor says he doesn't like to talk about his Marilyn Monroe days. But he will, from time to time, offer up more clues to the mystery of America's most glamorous female icon.

The adventure started one summer day in 1958, when Taylor's friend, playwright Arthur Miller, invited him to visit his home in Roxbury, Connecticut.

"Bring the kids," Miller suggested.

So Taylor loaded his four sons into the car and drove from New York City to the country house Miller shared with his famous wife, Marilyn Monroe. When they arrived, the playwright read aloud the first draft of a screenplay he titled *The Misfits.*

As Miller read, the drone of a vacuum cleaner, and the bumping, scraping sounds of housekeeping came from the second floor above them. Finally, the cleaning noises stopped. And then, a moment Taylor and his sons will never forget: Marilyn Monroe, her hair tied back, her face make-up free, lightly bounded down the stairs and into the room.

"She was a very pretty girl," Taylor says, and his eyes sparkle.

"Miller wrote *The Misfits* for Marilyn," Taylor explains. "She had said every one of the lines in the play. *The Misfits* is a true evocation of her beauty, her sensitivity, and her love for animals. I think she cared for animals more than she did for people."

At Marilyn's behest, Taylor became producer of *The Misfits*. At the beginning of their collaboration, Marilyn Monroe and Frank Taylor were great friends, deeply appreciative of the other's special qualities. But sadly, by the time the filming was done their relationship had crumbled. And so had her marriage to Arthur Miller.

So what was Marilyn Monroe really like?

"Marilyn had a need to seduce every man she met. Emotionally. Psychologically. Physically," Taylor explains. "She would unload her sad, ugly background on anyone she met, right at the beginning. She played on the sympathy of every person she encountered."

"She'd had a horrendous childhood. She really played on the waif thing. She made everyone feel protective of her. That's why women loved her, too."

But once she'd finished exposing her unhappy past, Taylor remembers, she got back to the business of being a movie star. She was an expert at it, a consummate professional. She took her job very seriously.

"She never appeared in public without make-up," Taylor says. "She did not have great legs, but she had great shoes, high heels that made her legs look great. She changed clothes at least five times a day. She couldn't bear the thought of disappointing her public."

Frank describes how Marilyn studied anatomy and learned how to pose her body at its very best. Every one of her gestures, every move she made, was studied, rehearsed. The way

Marilyn walked, sat, rose, and disembarked from a plane, was practiced. The way she tilted her pelvis, bent her ankle, carried her spine and ribs, all spoke of her understanding of her own physique.

"She wasn't showing off," Taylor explains. "She was being a star. She delivered."

As he reminisces, Frank Taylor's admiration of Marilyn Monroe is obvious. Evident too, is his sadness - vague, shapeless, but unmistakable.

"I loved her," he says finally. "All men did."

So why couldn't America's most dazzling star find happiness? Why could no one save her?

"She had no self-esteem at all," Taylor says. "It was the problem with all her relationships. They foundered on the fact that she felt she was not a worthy person, or even a good actress. Eventually that lack of self-worth transferred from her to you. It poisoned everything."

"But oh, when you were with her," Frank says, "she made you feel like a prince."

Jack Burke, The Key West Citizen

'Prisoners' After All

Were Beatles Cooped Up In Key West? No, No, No

SEP 12 1964

By DON EDIGER
Key West Bureau Chief

KEY WEST — The Bea-
tles, while pretending to be
couped up in a luxury motel
cottage, have actually been
sneaking out to get a look at
the Florida Keys, their press
secretary said Friday.

Press Secretary Derek Taylor, who for a time was forced
to shut off his phone — even
to the press — said all but
Ringo Starr have managed to
get past the legions of teenagers who have surrounded
their cottage.

"Except for Ringo they've
all gone out in cars at one
time or another," Taylor said.
Beatles were diverted
...ast from Toronto
...n Hurricane
...ding in

headed for a concert.
The Beatles wanted to go
to Nassau but settled for a
two days' rest here before
heading back to Jacksonville.

"John (Lennon) went shop-
ping in Key West Tr
and then drove up
Largo Thursday nig'
lor said.

He said George
and Paul (McCa
to the Sugarlo
dence of the Pa
Taylor g't
Ringo didn't :
looking arou

The Bea
manager,
earlier 1
been "1
motel
gum (

liked the area very much,"
Taylor said.
"But of course we've been
robbed here, too. It happens
wherever we go."

★ ★ ★

The kitchen staff at the Key
Wester was startled yesterday
at 5 p.m. when it received an
order from Ringo Starr for
"porridge."

After casting about to find out
just what porridge consists of,
it was decided that perhaps a
bowl of oatmeal would fill the
bill.

Sure enough it did — and so
it is assumed that for high tea,
Ringo likes oatmeal.

★ ★ ★

The Key Wester could probably make a fortune after the
Beatles leave if the manage-
ment would just sell off all the
furnishings, and practically any
thing the lads have touched.

Manager Fran Cuthbertson
says she has had offers to buy
the ashtrays, glasses — almost
any little piece of equipment
from the rooms. But the one
that really got her was a long
distance call from a woman who
wanted to send her a check to
cover the cost of the unlaundered sheets Ringo has slept on.

*The Beatles' first film, A Hard Day's Night,
was playing at the Strand Theater on
Duval Street in September, 1964, when
the Beatles visited Key West. According to
the director, Richard Lester, the film
"was based on their lives, living in small
boxes, as prisoners of their own success."*

A Hard Day's Night

You think you were lost in the '60s? Think how the people of Key West felt. As yet undiscovered, Key West was a lazy town back then, hot, slow, quiet and linked to the rest of the world by spotty media.

Then, on September 8, 1964, word came over the island's one radio station that the Beatles were coming. The Beatles were en route to a concert in Jacksonville when they were blown off course by Hurricane Dora. Key West was chosen as an ideal place for a two-day respite from the rigors of the road. Like the rest of the world, Key West was in the throes of Beatlemania. The band's movie *A Hard Day's Night* was playing at the Strand Theatre on Duval Street.

News of the Beatles expected arrival at Key West Airport spread across the island like a California forest fire. In no time every kid in town was headed for the airport, despite the fact that the band's plane was not scheduled to touch down till 4 a.m. It was a school night, but nobody cared about that either. A crowd of 700 fans stood vigil in the predawn haze.

Every Key West cop was there, whether officially on duty or not. Nonetheless, no one could persuade kids to come down off the roof of the airport.

Finally the plane touched down. The Beatles waved to the mob and jumped into Officer Nilo Albury's police cruiser for the short ride to the Key Wester Resort. Albury, uncle of two wildly smitten Beatlemaniac nieces, wisely took along his camera, a pen, and lots of paper for autographs. The Beatles, reportedly quite amiable, readily obliged.

Fans thronged the Key Wester Resort. They hid in the bushes. They stood in the grass and on the side of the road outside the Beatles' villa. Cops chased them away, and they returned moments later in search of better hiding places. For the length of their stay the fab four were forced to spend most of their time inside, ducking their frenzied fans.

After the Beatles swam in the Key Wester pool, a motel employee began selling tiny vials of "Beatle Water." Other employees sold the napkins, glasses, forks and knives used by the Beatles. A woman phoned the motel and begged to pay any price for Ringo's unlaundered sheets.

Key West cop Duke Yannaconne drove John Lennon and Paul McCartney to Leed's, a men's clothing store at 601 Duval Street. The boys bought socks and underwear.

"When we walked into the store," remembers Yannaconne, "the salesgirl fainted."

Somebody broke into the Beatle's villa and made off with several items of clothing. The Beatles didn't want to press charges, but they did want their clothes back. So Yannaconne placed an ad in the Key West Citizen offering amnesty to anyone coming forward with the stolen threads.

Meanwhile, a student at Key West High showed up selling tiny squares of a shirt that she claimed had up until very recently belonged to John Lennon. As proof, the girl flashed the shirt's collar with its identifying laundry mark.

Another student, an aspiring musician, turned up at school in Paul McCartney's collarless jacket. Within minutes officers arrived to take back the jacket and what remained of John Lennon's shirt.

As for the Beatles scrapbook with it's authentic autographs, photographs and many newspaper clips, Albury's nieces could never quite agree upon which of the two girls actually owned it. When the older of the sisters left town, she took the scrapbook with her. In 1984, short of cash, she sold it for $200.

Michael Keith

Mario Sanchez, on his twilight corner in Gato Village.
Mario was Florida's most famous folk artist and one of the last
surviving members of the society of Those Who Knew Hemingway.
He died in 2005, at the age of 96.

The Pope of Gato Village

O ur neighbor Thea teaches history in a high school up north nine months every year. She spends her summers in Key West in the house next door to ours. In the wintertime, from New Jersey she sends us chilling pictures of her northern home, buried in snow. She writes letters describing the long strings of dark days of her winter life, and her longing for her little house in Key West. When she arrives back in the summer, she calculates exactly how long it will be before she has to go back.

"I'm going to be here for the next 81 days," she said when arrived in June.

It's really fun, in a vicarious way, watching Thea discover and rediscover Paradise's many charms - the food, the little lanes, the layers of history, and the people. Re-acquainting herself with the island each summer, bit by tantalizing bit, Thea spends her time here in a sustained state of enchantment.

On the walls of her Key West home Thea has hung framed Mario Sanchez posters. Mario Sanchez is her favorite Key West artist.

'There is so much to see in each picture," she says. "The details are so wonderful. Mario Sanchez reminds me of all the things I love about this island."

Thea's favorite attraction is the East Martello Museum and Gallery. She visits the place often, stopping first, of course, in the Mario Sanchez exhibit. Mario's history lessons of Key West delivered by chunky little characters wearing brilliantly colored clothes beneath blue skies and puffy, white clouds on his carved and painted plaques of wood, speak volumes to Thea.

Yesterday, Thea arrived home from a shopping excursion excited and happy to have completed her collection of Mario Sanchez posters.

"I think I've got them all now," she said.

'Tonight," I said, "let's walk over to where Mario hangs and you can meet him."

In the cool of summer evenings, Mario and his brother Peruchio often sit on the corner of Catherine and Duval streets, in the heart of the neighborhood where both were born nearly 90 years ago. Mario was born in the second story of a place now called the Banana Cafe. The house where Peruchio was born is gone.

Their father was a reader in cigar factories. As the workers rolled cigars, Mr. Sanchez read to them from newspapers and novels in his famous, mellifluous voice. It made the time pass more quickly, and it was informative. He was the best reader on the island, Peruchio says. The brothers can tell you where the factories were located, the names of the men who owned them and the villages that developed around them. The village where Mario and Peruchio were born, where they sit today at sunset, was called Gato Village.

Peruchio is the talkative brother. Mario listens, and watches. His eyes are like a roving movie camera, exploring and preserving everything they see. When something in the conversation amuses Mario, he splays his strong thin fingers and claps his hands together gleefully, like a child. It seems a poignant gesture somehow, something important to remember. So I suggested to Thea that we hike over to the visit the Sanchez brothers on their twilight corner.

"Oh I couldn't," she said earnestly. "I would be tongue-tied. It would be like meeting God. "

"Of course it's like meeting God," I said. "He's an artist."

"It's better that I admire him from afar," Thea said reluctantly. "To me he's like the Pope."

"So come and meet a Pope," I said. 'The Pope of Gato Village."

Alan Maltz

Giving and Taking *is the name of this photograph by Alan Maltz.
It appears in his book, Key West Color. Unfortunately our friends lost
their copy before they got to see it, and to contemplate its message.*

The Sting

The last time my brother Rocky, who lives in New York, came to the Keys to do some fishing he brought along a buddy, Joe.

Naturally Joe fell in love with Key West. Ever since that visit, Joe's been planning his retirement in Paradise. Once in a while he phones to ask a question about something or other, We're always happy to answer it. Joe's a nice fellow and we certainly understand his passion for the island.

When it was time for Joe to get married, he decided to bring his fiance here to tie the knot. Sarah doesn't fish, but she likes to shop, and she was definitely ready to get married. In Key West. Or anywhere. Even before she'd been to the Keys, she agreed to retire here with Joe someday. She's pretty much willing to do wherever Joe asks her to do.

Rocky was invited to the wedding, but he wasn't too anxious to come here during the heat of summer. So when the Sarah wedding party, which consisted of Joe and Sarah, arrived in town, they phoned us. They were in a prenuptial daze, all goofy and excited. Joe invited us to go with them to dinner that night, but my husband Michael and I had recently decided to eliminate dining out from our routine as a cost-saving measure. Instead of going out for expensive meals, we decided we would buy expensive ingredients, stay home, and have our feasts our way.

"I'll cook dinner," I said to Joe, on the phone. "Come to our house and I'll fix you a welcome-to-Key West feast."

I prepared conch fritters. Jumbo peel-and-eat shrimp. Key lime pie with fresh-squeezed limes. And at every course, lots of stories and laughter about the vicissitudes of life in the tropics.

Sarah asked where we thought they should have their wedding dinner. She named a few places, but said that they were pretty set on Louie's Backyard.

"Whaddaya think?" Sarah asked. "Is the food good?"

"It's good and the place is beautiful," I said. "But it's awfully expensive."

"It's our wedding dinner," Sarah said. 'We don't care what it costs."

"So go to Louie's," I said. "Bon appetit."

I was feeling pretty pleased with myself as I cleaned up the monstrous mess I'd made, creating my local-color food sampler. We'd avoided a big dining out dent in our budget, and fulfilled our social obligations to my brother's fishing buddy and his fiance. We'd wished them a happy life, and sent them on their way.

The next day, Joe called to invite us to the wedding dinner. Another couple from New York had flown in for the wedding, and they would be at the party, too. Yes, it would be at Louie's, because they wanted it to be great. And they really, really wanted us to be there.

Louie's? We bought Alan Maltz's spectacular $50 coffee table book, Key West Color as a wedding gift. What a way to remember a Key West wedding. What a way to say "thanks for taking us to dinner at the most expensive restaurant in town."

The newest members of the party, a couple named Jack and Tina, battled throughout the wedding dinner about a misunderstanding they'd had at the Miami Airport hours earlier.

Do you see what you're signing on for, Joe?" Jack said, while his wife cursed all men for making all women miserable.

"It starts in Catholic school, when you keep us dumb and ugly in stupid uniforms and clodhopper shoes," his wife Tina said bitterly.

Over dessert and coffee, which Joe insisted we should all order, I thanked God that I'd escaped from New York. When the bill came and Joe and Sarah came out of their love cloud and studiously examined it.

"June and Michael don't drink, so they only owe $100," Joe said.

I choked on my decaf and Michael handed over his credit card.

The next day Joe phoned us from the airport.

"Time for the long ride home," he said regretfully.

"Take the Alan Maltz back on the plane with you," I said. It's very entertaining.

"Yeah. I can't believe Sarah left it under her chair at Sloppy Joe's last night!" Joe said. "Hey, maybe you can get another one and send it to us?"

"Yeah, maybe," I said. "Hey, bon voyage! Have a good life!"

*Sophie and Tessa. One of the great joys of our lives
in Key West has been our friendship with these remarkable little
Conch sisters. Now I know what Michael knew on that
golden day when the two girls met. And they do, too.*

Love at First Sight

The phone rang at 1:30 a.m. "It's time, Aunt June," Michael said jubilantly, turning on the light and hurrying me out of bed. We were going to Jenny and Rob's house to stay with their daughter Sophie, and they were going to the hospital to deliver Baby Tessa.

We arrived moments later to find Jenny sitting upright and wide-eyed on the couch. She was smiling her half-mysterious, half-triumphant, pregnant mother's smile. As Jenny waited, poised and ready for life's most joyful drama, we heard Rob, rummaging about in the rooms upstairs.

"What's he doing?" I asked. "Putting on a tuxedo?"

"If this isn't it, and they send me back home," Jenny said with a beautiful smile, "will someone please just shoot me?"

Just like being a grandparent is better than being a parent, being the friend of someone pregnant is worlds better than being being pregnant yourself. As Jenny and Rob drove off into the night, Michael and I settled into the guest room bed. Michael fell asleep and snored happily while I, nervous as a cat, dreamed weirdly and woke often, in anticipation of Sophie's morning cries and the call from the hospital.

Tessa was born just before dawn. Hours later we took 20-month-old Sophie to meet her. Tessa, swaddled in a blanket, wore a tiny pink cap on her peach-fuzzy head. She slept peacefully as Rob lifted her into Michael's arms, and Sophie nuzzled her, cooed softly, and patted her wee sister's face.

"Gentle, Honey," I whispered to Sophie, as her sisterly pats grew more insistent.

Jenny watched, with a Madonna smile, as her daughters met for the first time. Rob snapped pictures. Tears rolled down Michael's face. I nervously hoped and prayed that Sophie wouldn't poke out one or both of Tessa's eyes.

I have been told that when my parents brought my baby brother Fred home from the hospital, I headed for his room with scissors, and explaining to my horrified mother that I was going to correct our new baby's anatomical inaccuracy. I planned to rid him of his extra appendage. Mom stopped me before I changed the course of human events.

"Michael and Sophie holded Baby Tessa," Sophie said happily, as we left the hospital.

Later that day, Michael eloquently described for me, as only a poet can, what he was feeling as he watched Sophie meeting her sister for the first time.

"It was life-affirming," he said. "Love at first sight. These girls will have a lifetime of love and sharing. A love that will last longer than we will, June. Ordained by the universe. It is an honor to witness that."

I hid the scissors.

Join us on the worldwide web at:
www.JuneKeith.com

The logo of island native Meredith Bollong's sweet store that celebrates love, family, and tradition at the southernmost point.

Love's Gotta Go
First Class

The other day, in anticipation of Valentine season, I asked my husband Michael to tell me about his first kiss.

"I don't remember anything before you," my Southern gentleman spouse replied. "Before you, it's all prehistoric."

And if that isn't romantic enough, he'll give me a card, too.

I particularly love Valentine's Day because for a week before and a week after, I get to wear my Valentine jewelry: a rhinestone heart from my husband, a tiny gold heart from my mom, and a very old heart pendant that belonged to my grandmother. It opens, and inside there are tiny photos of my great-grandparents. I love wearing red, too.

As a not very popular or outgoing little kid, I loved Valentine's Day because everyone in the second grade got a pile of Valentines on their desk - even the nerds like me. In high school, I had special contempt for girls who used tiny fat hearts to dot their i's. Now, I understand that I was jealous of

them because those girls were usually the ones who had all
the fun.

Back then, I had a cousin who painted a wee red heart on
her cheek every Valentine's Day, and a green shamrock in the
same place on St. Patrick's Day. Her artiness inspired great
derision on campus, and each year I was mortified to be related to her, and secretly in awe of her courage.

Meredith, the beautiful proprietress of a lovely gift shop
on Petronia St., grew up in Key West with a wonderful tradition. Every Valentine's Day, Meredith awoke to find a small
stack of beautifully wrapped gifts, labeled to her from "Guess
Who?" The Valentine Man brought them, while she was sleeping, her mother explained.

Meredith never understood why she had to go to school on
the holiday known as St. Valentine's Day. After all, every other
gifting holiday meant a day off. But she went, happy and
inspired by the special day, and when she got to school, she
excitedly asked her classmates: "What did the Valentine Man
bring you?"

"The who?" they asked.

Eventually, she learned to stop asking, but the tradition
continues in her family. The romance of the Valentine Man
may well have influenced Meredith, the adult, to create a gift
shop named after the Spanish song title, "Besame Mucho,"
which translates to "kiss me a lot!" The shop is full of amorous
gifts and romantic tokens, as well as evocative photos and
other memorabilia from her Key West childhood.

"This shop feels like a valentine to Meredith's family," my
romantic husband says.

My brother Rocky's birthday is so close to Valentine's Day
that I often decorate his gift box in the spirit of it. Last year,
I sent Michael to the post office with a gift box addressed to
Rocky in New York. The box was plastered with hearts and
cherubs, in honor of the season.

"This needs to go first class," Michael told Esther, at the Post Office counter.

"Oh yes," Esther agreed, smiling at the proliferation of hearts. "Love's gotta go First Class."

HARRY POWELL

Isaac Valdez

In this great Key West Resort
There's a park called Peary Court
Where the grass and weeds and
bougainvillea grows
But the Navy they did say
They gonna chop it all away
And fill it up with tacky bungalows
But Harry Powell, Harry Powell
let out a civic howl
Said I will not let them
do this to Key West
And with a strange smile on his face
He walked on the Navy base
with a case of dynamite strapped to his chest
He said someone's got to stop
This building boom and t-shirt shops
Cause this paradise is much too sweet to lose
So I'll keep this island green or blow us all to smithereens
And he stuck a match and held it to the fuse
And he said one-two-three-four you ain't gonna build no more
They yelled five-six-seven-eight go on Harry detonate
Oh Harry Powell, Harry Powell
Here comes the sheriff now
With the FBI and ninety deputies
Before you blew yourself to hell
They locked you in a prison cell
With your explosive personality
Now some say he's a criminal and some say he's insane
Because he would not throw in the towel
But we've gotta keep him free cause what will this island be
Without Peary Courts and Harry Powells
Oh Harry Powell, Harry Powell
Where are you now
'Stead of dynamite there's a number on your chest
But we'll keep this island green and fulfill the golden dream
Of Harry Powell, hero of Key West
— Shel Silverstein

Something
Wild About Harry

The last time I saw Harry Powell was right before Christmas. He came into the Lighthouse Cafe where I wait tables. He was with his wife, Dane, and a group of people I'd never met before. The restaurant was awfully busy that night, but I've waited on Harry and Dane before, and they're really nice.

"That's City Commissioner Harry Powell," I whispered to the hostess.

It hasn't always been this way. Back in the late '80s when Harry was a city commissioner and I was working for Mayor Richard Heyman, Harry and I often ended up on opposite sides of the political fence.

I was no seasoned politico, but I'd been working for the city for a few more years than Harry when he was elected. I, along with others at City Hall, made fun of his lack of political savvy. He was very, very green, and, like most newcomers to political office, absurdly idealistic.

Despite the derision, Harry quickly found his stride. He was the underdog's commissioner, who always had time to sit still and listen to somebody with a problem. No lost cause was truly lost until Harry had exhausted every possible avenue of salvation.

Harry's no stone unturned policy was evident at city commission meetings, too. For example, when Truman Annex proposed to build a series of affordable condominiums that would be available to working people of Key West, Harry was reluctant to waive the zoning laws that would allow for the Shipyard Condominiums.

"My fear is that people from up North will buy these units at very affordable prices and rent them out," Harry explained. "The working people of Key West will be left right back where they started - desperate for affordable housing."

But the commission was promised that deed restrictions on the condos would allow no such usage. And Harry was out-voted. A few short years down the road, it became obvious that Harry had been right about the future of the condominiums on Truman Annex.

When the U.S. Navy announced plans to plow under the baseball field and turn Peary Court into a housing development for recruits and their families, many in the city were outraged. Peary Court was an important part of Key West's culture. Commissioner Harry Powell jumped into the fray with the same intensity that he used for all battles. Right from the start he believed himself to be on the side of justice and fair play. He used his power and resources to shine a great big spotlight on the soft spots in the Navy's position.

Peary Court became Harry's consuming passion. He turned up evidence, policies and documents that supported his position. He worked the press. He went to Washington. He fought like a mad dog for what he believed was right for Key West. He kept up the fight even after he completed his term in office and went back to being a civilian.

One night when Harry was in the restaurant, I asked him about Peary Court. It was like lighting the fuse to a firecracker. Harry's eyes lit up as he eloquently outlined new facts and figures, new evidence that shored up his position that the new buildings on Peary Court were unnecessary.

Whether or not I agree With Harry about Peary Court is not the point here, however. The point is that I've learned to recognize Harry as a person deserving of respect. He has always been the same man, of course, only I was too quick to judge him. Too quick to fixate on his weaknesses rather than his strengths. That's politics.

In letting go of politics, which I had to do to let go of prejudice, I set myself up to learn a lot more about love. When word of Harry's bizarre stand-off at Peary Court traveled across the island like a wildfire, I was horrified. It turned out to be true. Barricaded in a trailer with explosives at the Peary Court construction site, Harry held out for 10 hours in a desperate attempt to stop the project. I feared for his safety. When news of his surrender came, I was relieved.

I care about former Commissioner Harry Powell. I appreciate his passion, and on a deeper level, I approve of his madness.

Tennessee Williams, upon moving into his Key West digs.

Tennessee Williams Time

I
t's Tennessee Williams time in Key West. At the
Waterfront Theatre, Key West's resident famous actress,
Kelly McGillis, is starring in Williams's play *The Night of the
Iguana.* A couple doors down from the theater, at the the
Custom House Museum, there is an exhibit of Tennessee
Williams' paintings and a loving and thought-provoking
French documentary about Williams's life and work. A work-
shop was recently organized to study Williams's plays. Lately,
newspaper reporters are coming to Key West from near and
far, in search of new angles on the old stories about the man
who, during his lifetime, was reverently, and rightfully, called
"America's greatest living playwright."

Tennessee Williams arrived in Key West for the first time in
1941 as a struggling playwright. He was 30 years old. In the
next decade *The Glass Menagerie* and *A Streetcar Named Desire*
made him rich and successful beyond his wildest dreams.
Fame and fortune enabled Williams to travel and live wherev-

er and however he pleased. He chose Key West. In 1950, he bought a cozy house on Duncan Street. He added a pool, and a writing studio. In his memoirs Williams said that although he wrote in many places, he did his best writing in the studio of his Key West house.

In spite of his great talent, it seems Key West has never embraced Williams the way it has Ernest Hemingway. The reason for that is simple, says Key West writer Leigh Rutledge. America cherishes Hemingway because he represents all that is desirable in masculinity: power, aggression, daring and courage. Hemingway was a hunter, a fisherman, a boxer, an avid fan of bullfighting, a man married four times. Williams, on the other hand, was a timid man, small of stature and somewhat delicate. He was gay. As a writer he was profoundly aware of the comedic, tragic ruts and twists of human nature. This eternal balancing act of man's emotions formed the basis of his important work. America is proud of men like Hemingway, Rutledge says, and sort of embarrassed of men like Williams.

When he was in his sixties, Williams took up painting, under the tutelage of renowned Key West artist Henry Faulkner. Painting, Williams said, did not wear him out like writing did. (Faulkner's wonderful rendition of the Hemingway House hangs still over the bed in the master bedroom at the Hemingway House.) Williams gave his images fantastic names like "Fairy in a Wicker Chair"; "Great Silence of the Storm"; "Many Moons Ago"; and "Recognition of Madness."

Tennessee Williams died in 1983, in the Hotel Elysee, in New York City. When word of his death reached Key West, the film version of Williams's play *The Rose Tattoo*, began playing at the Key West Picture Show, a chic alternative cinema on Duval Street. The film was packed for every viewing.

The house on Duncan Street remained vacant for many

years after Williams's death. A group of writers joined forces
to have the property turned into a sort of shrine to the writer,
but the memorial was not to be. The house was sold in 1992
and completely refurbished. The re-do included a high, white
fence to keep out curiosity seekers.

Several people I know who have seen the current produc-
tion of *The Night of the Iguana* here in Key West say that from
it they glean that Williams as a very angry man. Maybe he was
by 1960, when the play was originally produced. Depressed by
the death of his long-time companion Frank Merlo, and suffering from what he called "the tragedy of success," Williams
drank and pilled way too much. By then, critics say, he had
begun to lose his fine edge. The flame that was Williams's
great light began to flicker long before it finally extinguished
for good.

I never met Tennessee Williams, but like many longtime
Key Westers I have heard the stories about him, his sweetness,
his charm, his madness, and his paranoia. The Tennessee
Williams I love and cherish is the young man who wrote *The
Rose Tattoo*, a story about love and passion and betrayal and
survival, and all those great themes Williams fleshed out so
brilliantly. It is Williams's only play with a happy ending, and
when it became a movie in 1955, it was filmed here, on this
then-remote island that Williams called home.

On the day Williams died, I went with friends to the Key
West Picture Show. We crowded into the theater, sat through
two showings of *The Rose Tattoo*, and thanked God for
Tennessee Williams.

Michael Keith

My baby brother Rocky keeping me warm on the Digby/St. John Ferry,
in the Canadian Maritimes. There's a real chill in that ocean wind,
and I'm feeling it, but Rocky is conditioned by many early
New England mornings in the garbage truck to function
well in the most challenging weather.

Stick Out Your Can

My brother Rocky, the garbage man, and I have a regular telephone routine. I say, "How's business, Rocky?" and he says "Pickin' up."

Then I say, "Stick out your can. Here comes the garbage man."

I've spent the last week at Rocky's little house in New York. Rocky retires every night at 10, and arises at 5:30 a.m. Sometimes I join him in greeting the day. He's always in a very good mood in the morning, cracking jokes and telling stories as he fixes his coffee, feeds Willy, the cat, and asks me if I am having a good vacation. I am. Then, he leaves for work. And I go back to bed.

Rocky's garbage truck is a noisy gargantua, a modern miracle of gears and hydraulics that Rocky spent his childhood preparing to operate. As a little kid, Rocky's favorite toys were trucks and cars. He loved playing in the dirt and gravel with little pickup trucks with working tail gates, dump trucks that really dumped, cranes that really lifted. He loves bulldozers. When he could reach the pedals, he graduated to little cars, and then motorized go-carts, and then, a mini-bike, the pre-cursor to his beloved Harley-Davidson of current times.

Driving a garbage truck is a perfect job for a large motor vehicle enthusiast. Picking up trash works, too, because Rocky grew up to be a very big, very powerful guy, and you need a big, strong guy to pick up garbage. Rocky never completely shed the rebelliousness of his youth. It's a very good job for a rebel.

"Nobody tells me what to do. I'm my own boss," Rocky says. "I get the job done."

On Rocky's longest route, every Monday, he makes 420 stops. At each stop, he slides out of the driver's seat of Gargantua, the garbage truck, drops down to the earth, and hopes no one will run him down as he is doing his job, pouring garbage cans full of trash into Gargantua's grimy jaws.

Being a garbage man is documented as one of the most dangerous occupations in America. Cars passing by just don't want to stop or slow down or wait for the garbage man to do his job.

"Your house makes garbage, too, right?" Rocky says to people who whiz past him, gesturing obscenely, yelling rudely, or berating him for holding up the world.

Another hazard is the recent advent of bigger garbage cans. A couple of years ago Rocky asked me to help him write a letter to Rubbermaid, explaining to them their new jumbo, 45-gallon garbage cans, were creating a serious challenge to garbage men everywhere.

In spite of the hazards, Rocky loves his job. His customers love him, and so do their kids. Even the dogs are happy to see him. Rocky carries dog biscuits. At Christmas time, he picks up trash in a Santa Claus suit.

Last week, one of Rocky's customers told him her husband had died days earlier.

"What did you say?" I asked.

"What could I say? I hugged her and told her I was sorry," he said.

About a year ago, Rocky's perfect world was knocked off it's orbit when he lifted one of those new 45-gallon garbage pails and felt something snap deep inside his shoulder. He hasn't been the same since. For months, he bullishly continued to do his job, in spite of the pain. He submitted to a surgical procedure that ultimately failed. He has limited mobility in his right arm. The pain is constant. Nowadays, Rocky drives Gargantua and is assisted in picking up by a helper named Eddie. He has lost his cherished independence.

The surgeon offered to declare Rocky permanently disabled, assuring him disability payments, or retraining for another type of work. But Rocky doesn't want disability checks or a new career. He wants to continue being everybody's favorite garbage man.

I don't think Rocky's boss, friends and family grasp the magnitude of his tragedy, or imagine the depth of his pain. I don't think they know, because I don't think they understand the fullness of his happiness, his satisfaction in being one absolutely fantastic garbage man.

Mimi McDonald

Did you know children's book author Shel Silverstein
wrote "On the Cover of the Rolling Stone" and "A Boy Named Sue"?
Here he is at Captain Tony's Saloon surrounded by Key West
friends (left to right) Baby Courtney Krumel, Linda and
Chuck Krumel, Ritchie Krumel, Shel, Gary McDonald,
Toni Tarracino, Captain Tony and Susan Nadler.

This Rock Won't Roll

My brother Rocky is a man of few words. Nonetheless, he phones me regularly. Now that he is a grown adult, aged 30-something with a job and a phone bill of his own, he no longer calls me collect from phone booths in the furtive predawn hours. Nowadays, he calls way before bedtime.

Yesterday, Rocky called to say he's considering a move to the Florida Keys. The woman with whom he has shared his life the past 15 years, the woman whose name is emblazoned across his heart in a glorious red, purple and blue tattoo, has grown silent and untouchable.

"What do you think is the problem?" I asked.

"Eh, I don't know," my baby brother answered.

We do not have in-depth conversations. We never have. Time with Rocky is spent listening to music, or watching television, or driving through the beautiful New England back roads where we grew up.

Last fall I visited Rocky. To demonstrate the stunning capabilities of his new stereo he played the song "On The Cover Of The Rolling Stone."

"I bought this whole CD just to get this one song," he said.

"Shel Silverstein wrote this song," I said excitedly, suddenly spotting an inroad to conversation. "He lives in Key West!"

"Oh yeah?" Rocky said.

We were eating takeout pizza and I, ever hungry for possible topics of conversation with my elusive brother, commented on how good it tasted.

"I don't know why," Rocky said, "but there is no pizza anywhere as good as what you get here. Outside of Connecticut, New York and New Jersey I've never had a good pizza. I don't know why that is. The humidity? Something in the water? I wonder about that."

I was struck dumb. It was the longest speech I had ever heard him make.

One of Rocky's hobbies is ice fishing. He likes photography, too. Last year he sent me a self-portrait of himself posing on the ice, dressed in a thermal jumpsuit. In it he looks like a big, brown polar bear, patient and content, the only living thing on a long, lonely expanse of white snow and ice.

Two winters ago he sent me pictures of his new house, a sweet little cottage in the middle of the woods, with a chimney and a stone wall surrounding it. Since Rocky bought his own house I always ask him during our telephone conversations how things are going with it.

"We had to put on a new roof," he told me during a call a month ago.

"Wow, that sounds like a big job," I said.

"Eh, it was all right," he answered.

Lately, Rocky has been calling more frequently than usual to discuss his moving plans. I am thrilled with the prospect of having my baby brother within hugging distance again.

"Maybe we'll get a bigger house and we can all live together," I suggested.

"I think I'll live up the Keys a ways," Rocky said apologetically. "Maybe I'll buy a little tackle shop and live upstairs. "

"And what about your house in New York? Will you sell it?" I asked.

"Eh, maybe," he replied.

"You can put your Harley in the back of your Blazer and drive down," I suggested.

"If I still have the Blazer by then," Rocky said.

"By when?" I asked.

"About two years," Rocky said.

'Two years!" I exclaimed.

"Rocky, I thought you were coming now."

"No. Not now," he said. "Some day. But I'm coming."

So is Eli. So is Godot.

The Fabulous Spectrelles. What woman wouldn't kill to be transformed for just one night into a sloe-eyed doll with the kind of behind designers had in mind when they invented Spandex?

Walking In The Sand

The other day I was at my girlfriend Sally O'Boyle's house, waiting while she tended to her rambunctious 4 and 5-year-old boys, when I spotted a teasing comb and a jumbo-sized can of Final Net hairspray on the dining room table.

"Girlfriend!" I said. "1 didn't know you teased your hair. I thought that snarl was an accident."

"Oh, I haven't told you yet," Sally laughed, tossing her regally red head. "I'm a Fabulous Spectrelle now! I tease my hair into a big beehive every night!"

I almost fainted with envy.

"Can I try your false eyelashes?" I asked weakly. "Is it fun being a Spectrelle?"

"It's the best fun in the world," Sally said, grinning as if it was 1966 and we were getting away with something big.

If there really is such a thing as reincarnation, I want to live my next life in the body of a narrow-kneed girl with a great voice and big hair. The next me will look terrific in eye-liner, harmonize like an angel and sashay with the smokey grace of a Brooklyn slut. I will sing back-up doo wop in spiked heels, and, because I will never even think of trying for lead, every other girl in the group will be my friend.

Just a mention of the Fabulous Spectrelles, Key West's own retro girl group, and the fantasy center in my brain is off and running, churning vampish visions to the rhythms of doo ron ron. And I'm not the only one. I know dozens of women on this island who would gladly give up their off-street parking places to spend a night crooning and shaking their booties with the Fabulous Spectrelles. Who wouldn't kill to be transformed, just for one night, into a sloe-eyed doll with the kind of behind that the designers had in mind when they invented Spandex?

Being a Spectrelle answers Sally's lifelong dream of being on stage. Performing, and foraging for the next opportunity to perform, up until recently has been the prime focus of her life. In a way that perhaps only other performers can really understand, my friend Sally is most alive, her truest self, in front of an audience.

"I always wanted to be a big star," Sally says. "I wanted to marry Sean Penn and have an apartment in New York and a house in L.A."

Eight years ago she went to New York for one final shot at fame. For a year she concentrated on doing nothing but whatever it would take to land a role in a Broadway show, or a Hollywood film. But no part materialized. And in the course of giving it her all, she realized that she was no longer willing to devote her life to the tantalizing and ever-frustrating pursuit of stardom. She wanted something different, something surer.

"Today I'm married to a middle-aged Republican with a job," she laughs. "He's not Sean Penn, but . . . he's Mr. Right. Marriage and children have changed my life in ways I'd never imagined would happen to me."

Still, she says, there's this need for the spotlight that will never go away. It's a pleasure button in her personality that can only be pushed by performing. From time to time, there's a role in a play, or a temporary singing gig - like this one with the Spectrelles - and the actress/singer inside of her gets a life-affirming dose of validation.

'The other day I told my husband, 'you know how good you feel when your golf score is 80? That's how I feel when I'm on stage with the Spectrelles singing "Walking in the Sand."

When Sally, daytime mother and real estate broker, night-time doo ron diva, dons her pantyhose, big hair, eye-liner, false eyelashes, and her '60s-era dresses, her little boys watch in fascination. They run their hands over her legs encased in nylon and they giggle.

"Oh Mom, you're so cool," they tell her, and Sally's heart bursts with a different kind of happiness.

"Performing used to be my everything," Sally says. "Now it's the icing on the lovely cake that is my life."

June Keith

The writer Dilys Winn, founder of a New York City book shop called "Murder Ink." Dilys is a recipient of the prestigious Edgar Award for mystery writing, and there is an annual award named for her. When I had trouble trying to remember the spelling of her name she told me to remember it like this: Darling I Love You So.

We'll Die For You

After watching a couple friends perform in a campy, interactive whodunit parlor game at Miss Marble's Parlor and Mystery Book Shop, I suggested to shop owner Dilys Winn that if she ever needed a big blond, I was available. Her bright eyes, aglow with a glimmer of lunacy, turned neon when I said my husband would act, too.

Finally, our chance came. Last week Dilys called and asked us to appear in one of her zany dramas. I would play a whorish psychic. Michael would be a nerdy IRS agent. Were two roles ever so clearly ours? All we had to do, Dilys explained, was enter the parlor at 8 p.m., clutch our throats, stagger like poisoned people dying hideous deaths might do, and - die. Easy enough.

"Sure," I told Dilys. 'We'll die for you."

Dilys sent me to the Knot So New Consignment Shop where Ilene, the shop owner, who really is psychic, handed me dress after whorish dress to try, while a salesgirl named Lucy and I discussed the meaning of the word "whore." Does a

whore get paid a lot for sex, or simply have a lot of sex? I say
the second. Please don't ask me why.

After I'd found my costume, a tight green and gold skirt
with a giant flounce in a shimmery fabric, with a matching
leopard-skin print jacket, I was to report to Dilys for costume
approval.

"Here are my corpses now," Dilys said to someone on the other
end of the phone, when Michael and I walked into her shop.

Dilys loved my costume, and was so encouraged by our
enthusiasm for acting, she made an impulsive decision to
expand our roles. After our death scenes, according to the
new script, we were to quickly change into angels' wings and
choir robes. Oblivious to anyone else but our ghostly selves,
Michael and I were to wander around, discussing bright white
lights at the end of a tunnel. We were also to drop occasional
clues.

Late Friday afternoon, while I teased my hair and applied
a half-pound of make-up, Michael hunted for the gray flannel
suit he'd stashed in the back of his closet 10 years ago. While
he knotted his tie, I parted his hair down the middle and plastered it with gel. We found his old briefcase.

At 7:30, we headed on foot for the mystery theater, with
absolutely no clue of how our appearance on Duval Street
would affect sunset pedestrians. Michael, the nerd in the suit
and tie carrying a briefcase, and I, his whorish companion in
the leopard skin suit, jangley jewelry and cheap perfume, created a bona fide scene.

"Is this your first blind date?" I shrilled to Michael as we
passed a group of pedestrians. Some polite types tried hard to
not stare. Others glared at me disapprovingly. "How do you
like Key West so far?" I shouted gaily, as Michael managed to
stay in poker-faced character.

A girl sitting on the sidewalk stared hard, and then when
we were past, sighed loudly and gasped "My nerves," as if she'd

hallucinated us.

Soon, it was 8 o'clock. Showtime! As we waited in the wings, with the other, more seasoned cast members, Dilys appeared to give us some last minute directions.

"When you do your death scenes, really camp them up," she said to us. "You should really overact, and don't worry about looking foolish."

Then, as a sort of afterthought, Dilys murmured, "I could never do what you're about to do."

But Michael and I had no qualms about looking foolish, and no fears of losing our dignity. Our impromptu dress rehearsal on Duval Street had cured us of all that.

Baking with Tessa and Sophie. Thanks for inspiring us, Martha!
Our cakes aren't perfect but we're proud of them and
they tasted delicious.

It's a Good Thing

My husband loves Martha Stewart. Every night, at 11 p.m., he watches her television show. We discovered Martha by accident one restless night a few weeks ago. And now we never miss her.

"Who is this woman?" Michael said, on that first night, suddenly sitting straight up in bed in rapt attention, as Martha assembled a trellis in the back yard of her New England country house.

He thinks Martha is a model woman. He likes her clothes. He likes her hair. He likes her ideas. He's mad for her kitchen and her strawberry pots and her baked apples that make the whole house smell like a Currier and Ives Christmas.

His favorite Martha Stewart program so far was the making preserves show. Michael is the kind of guy who gets lost in the jams and jellies aisle at the grocery store. The more expensive and exotic the blend, the more likely it is to spend the next 2 years of its life in our refrigerator. But no more. From now on, we're making our own.

"Think of the possibilities," Michael says. "Key limes. Mango. Guava."

And as a result of my husband's new fascination with Martha Stewart we no longer buy fresh picked herbs. We grow them ourselves, on our back deck. Like Martha.

"She's very earthy. Even when her hands are covered in dirt, Martha is able to maintain her elan," Michael says. "Not too many woman can do that."

This weekend we're painting flower pots. Martha and Michael are tired of terra cotta.

Michael believes that watching something creative like the *Martha Stewart Show,* just before you go to sleep, is good for your imagination.

"From every show you get four great ideas," Michael says. "Then, while you're sleeping you process the information. It's a good thing."

Sometimes Michael falls asleep midway through Martha's show. The next morning, of course, he begs me to tell him what he missed.

"Martha was real earthy last night," I told him the other day. "She made sandwiches out of ingredients from her garden — baby lettuce, basil leaves, and cherry tomatoes. Then she slaughtered this cute pig she'd raised in a pen next to the compost heap. After she butchered Pork Chop — that was the little pig's name — she made smoked ham for the sandwiches."

"Wow," Michael said, turning pale. "I'm glad I missed that."

"I had nightmares," I said.

Recently I came across Martha Stewart's biography on the Internet. Martha is from New Jersey, made a killing in the stock market, and owns several country homes. She and Michael are the same age. Martha was married, but her husband left her to run off with a woman 30 years younger.

These facts I dutifully reported to Michael, who seemed saddened by the news of Mr. Stuart's betrayal.

"She won't have what Martha has," Michael said ruefully.

"Right," I said. "She's 30 years younger."

"You think it's easy to talk to a 25-year-old woman?" Michael said.

"I don't think talk is necessarily what he's looking for," I said.

Then, at 10:55 p.m., I switched off the television and turned out the lights.

"Hey!" Michael yelled. "What are you doing?"

"No Martha Stewart tonight, honey," I said. "We need to talk."

Susan Pitts

*US 1 begins in Ft. Kent, Maine and ends here, at the
Monroe County Court House, where the fact is commemorated
with this sign, a favorite tourist photo opportunity.*

Judge Judy Duty

When the summons to jury duty came in the mail, I was thrilled and honored to be called. I immediately did the paper work and sent it back the court. Yes, I could and certainly would make it.

Tell people you're scheduled for jury duty and they wince and moan and pat you on the back with pity, as if you've announced you're being audited by the IRS.

"You can get out of it," they say. "Just tell them you hate guns. Or cops. Or people. Act meek and indecisive. They'll let you go."

"But I don't want to get out of it," I told a compassionate friend. "I want to be a juror."

"My God, that's commendable of you," he said, and I swear I saw tears glistening in his eyes.

Last Monday morning, I walked to the courthouse and signed in at exactly 8:30 a.m. The crowd was quite spectacular and so full of familiar faces I wondered who was still out there in the world shopping, doing laundry, and walking on the sidewalks. It seemed that everybody I'd ever seen in Key West had been called to jury duty.

There were barely enough seats to accommodate the masses. I found a seat next to an attractive guy wearing a musky cologne so intense within seconds it began to feel like a parade of invisible ants with feathery feet were climbing into my nostrils. Before the sneezing fit started I jumped up and moved far from the offending scent.

I resettled into another seat near my former allergy man, Dr. Al Bowen. We exchanged greetings across the guy who sat between us.

"I think I should warn you people that I'm just getting over a horrible cold," the guy between us said. "I don't know whether or not I'm still contagious."

At 9:30 the judge arrived, cloaked in black robes and exuding glorious pomp. With our right hands in the air, we the people swore to state the truth in his courtroom.

"I swear that I am over 18," the judge said.

"Yes," the crowd responded in unison.

"I swear that the summons for jury duty was issued in my correct name," the judge said.

"Yes," the potential jurors said.

"I swear I am a citizen of the United States," he said.

I raised my hand, and a football field-sized courtroom of eyes turned my way.

"I'm not a U.S. citizen," I told the judge. "I'm married to an American. I've been a legal alien since I was 3. I am a citizen of Canada."

"Then you are dismissed," the judge said. "If you want to serve on a jury you have to go to Canada."

I nearly cried. The first one sent home, and the one most willing to serve.

There is a reason why I'm not an American by now. It's about health insurance, and how, as a writer, I've mostly lived without it. In Canada, health care is free to citizens, even the ones crazy enough to be writers or actors or artists.

I made it home just before the rain came. As thunder rumbled and lightening lit up the skies, I tuned into my favorite morning TV show, Judge Judy. Suddenly, the power snapped off and I was ejected from Judge Judy's courtroom, too.

The people rested.

Strawberry picking in Nova Scotia. Summer, '05.

Michael Keith

Quiet! It's the Universe!

When my friend Rene, the consignment shop entre-
preneur, lost the lease at the marina where she
docks her houseboat, and couldn't find another
slip for rent anywhere, she told me that she was considering
what the universe was trying to tell her.

"I think it may be time for me to leave Key West," Rene
said.

My heart clutched. Rene's shop is one of my favorite hang-
outs. What would I do without her? And her giant closet full
of recycled goods. I appealed to her sense of logic.

"So when Rick, my hair dresser, told me he was leaving the
business because of his carpal tunnel syndrome, the universe
was telling me I should no longer have sun-kissed blonde
highlights in my hair?" I said. "Of course not. Rick Brady may
retire, but Lady Clairol is forever."

My logic did not impress. The universe was sending Rene
a message, and the harder she listened, the clearer that message became. A few days later, Rene told me her houseboat

and her store were on the market. The universe had spoken.

I began to wonder if the universe had sent messages to me, that I had consistently missed. (You find yourself thinking this way a lot when you turn 50.) Perhaps I am living a life absolutely opposite from the one the universe would have me live. Maybe I'm supposed to be a country woman, back in Nova Scotia, with 6 kids and 10 grandchildren, picking berries, making pies, watching TV via a satellite dish in my backyard, and playing Bingo at the legion hall on Wednesday nights.

I voiced these concerns to my husband, who listened with his usual amazing and profound patience, and I reflected that the universe had tossed me a bonus when they crossed my path with his.

"Michael," I said, "How do you know the difference between a random twist of fate and a message from the universe?"

We agreed to pay more attention to the universe. And sure enough, there were messages everywhere. The tricky part is interpreting them.

Dog-sitting for my mom's Pekingese, for example, has given us a clear message: we are not little-dog people. But when I pulled my hamstring in yoga class, the message was not so clear. Is yoga not kosher? Should I be doing Tae Bo?

"You know you're the only man who's ever truly understood me and my vanity," I told Rick, last Saturday, the final time he did my hair. "I don't know how I'm going to survive without you."

Rick told me that he was going to sell appliances at Sears and if I wanted to buy a new refrigerator or stove, I should definitely buy it from him. Then, he explained to me why using a dishwasher was actually more ecologically efficient than washing dishes by hand.

Aha!

A message from the universe.

"We need to buy a dishwasher," I told Michael when I got home. "I got the message a little while ago."

Sunday morning, Michael took Babe, our Pekingese house guest, along on his walk to get the Sunday papers. Just as they were walking past Valladares news store, a zebra finch flew into the window, knocking itself unconscious. Then, a black and white, three-legged cat and Babe, the nervous Pekingese, enjoyed a delicate, but ultimately favorable encounter as Michael cradled the tiny bird in his hand until it came to its senses and flew away.

"What do you suppose the universe was telling us this morning?" he asked.

"Why can't we all just get along?" I suggested.

"Or maybe, sometimes just trying to get along is like banging your head against a wall," he said.

Michael Keith

Sharing a moment with Michael's brother, talking head
Kenley Jones of NBC News.

Talking Head Widow

For months I've been looking forward to Election Day. I've been ready to get the matter of who our next president will be settled for a long, long time. No other campaign in history has so impinged upon my personal life more than this one. It's because my husband Michael, usually the best companion a girl could hope to find, is a campaign junkie. I have lost him to Tim Russert. Our lives are scheduled around *Meet the Press* and *Hardball* and *Larry King Live* and CNN news updates. I awaken each day to Don Imus interviewing somebody or other, and fall asleep each evening as Michael is logging on to late-night Internet for some fresh clue as to who our next president will be.

And I've been very patient throughout all of this. After all, this is a man who went to a good college and even majored in history. Foreign as that seems to me, I am proud of his intellect, and his vast knowledge of Why Things Are The Way They Are. for many years he has been filling in the blanks, and connecting the dots in my own sketchy understanding of

America's past.

On Tuesday night I went to bed giddy with anticipation of getting my husband back, as he sat before the television, busily pushing the remote control buttons, with occasional dashes to the bathroom to splash cold water on his face to keep himself awake.

"Don't come to bed until you have good news for me," I whispered as I kissed him good night.

At 3 a.m. I awakened to find him in bed next to me. That he hadn't waked me with the news that my candidate had won did not bode well. I slipped into the living room, turned on the TV, and heard the terrible news. The election was not yet settled, and the talking heads were flummoxed. The candidates' representatives were hoarse and bleary-eyed as they responded to still more interviews with the CNN gang.

By 7 a.m. the following morning, Michael was back in front of the TV, waiting for the winner to be announced. And that's where he's been, pretty much, since Election Day.

"This is history in the making," he tells me. "One day we'll be telling our grandkids about this."

"Oh, and they'll be fascinated, I'm sure," I said. "'Gramps! Tell us about Election 2000, when you watched TV for four whole months straight!'"

It has occurred to me that the "Survivor" show, the one that kept people glued to their sets each week last spring, was a sort of warm-up for this presidential election. Who will have the tenacity to prevail? I have been watching a soap, "All My Children", for years, and I know how much fun it is to be entertained with outlandish stories full of shakily constructed counter-plots. Perhaps those talking heads got together and decided to orchestrate an enormous fraud, a national trick, to see how long they could keep America on the edge of its seat.

Nowadays, when Michael chides me about my devotion to "All My Children", I rebuke him for his love affair with CNN.

"Who writes this crap?" Michael says incredulously, as my soap opera characters deal with betrayals and lost libidos and fraudulent pregnancies at 1 p.m. each day.

"Who writes this crap?" I now say, as the Vice President gabs on and on about the constitution and the complexities of the electoral college system, and his opponent shrills of his eminent victory.

"I just want my husband back!" I moaned to my brother Rocky on the phone yesterday.

"So run for office," he advised.

My Jersey girlfriends staying cool. Teacher and summertime neighbor Thea Hyde (left) and writer, fulltime islander, Jennifer O'Lear, hanging out.

The Dawn-Busters

It's 4 a.m., and next door, there's a party going on. The neighbors have just returned from work. They make their livings waiting on tables, or tending bar, and by this time of the night—or the day, depending on how you look at things—they have plenty to talk about. This is their cool-down time, the hour between the dusk and the dawn when harried waitrons and service workers unwind after a night of running, fetching, serving, and putting up with God only knows what new outrage each evening.

The young man and woman have plenty of friends, apparently in the same business. It is customary for them to assemble on the deck behind their house, regardless of the temperature. On those bitterly cold mornings in December, they were out there, yakking away, impervious to the cold that kept us huddled under a heap of ancient blankets.

They do not play loud music, or turn on the TV. They only talk. But their talk seems to enrage the neighborhood chickens, who crow incessantly at the low rumble of conversation breaking into the wee hours that usually belong exclusively to them.

Michael and I, former service industry workers ourselves, do not begrudge our neighbors their cool-down hour. We understand totally. What frustrates me is that while their conversation is enough to keep me awake, it is not loud enough to understand clearly. I cannot make out the words. From time to time there are loud exclamations like: "NO! I DON'T BELIEVE IT!" or "SHE SAID THAT?" Meanwhile, I lie in my bed, straining my ears to hear the details. What unbelievable thing did someone do? What did that bitchy customer say? One of the perks of waiting on tables is being ever amazed and astounded at how outrageously boorish seemingly normal people can sometimes be. I miss the cool-down gossip. I want to hear just how bad things have become since I left the business. But, I can't. The neighbors don't talk loud enough.

The house next door is a cigarmakers cottage, like ours. Only six or so feet of alley separate us, and, on very quiet nights it is actually possible to hear a person in the next house sneeze or walk down the hall to the bathroom. After many years here, we are accustomed to this island intimacy.

Thea, the owner of the house, is a school teacher in New Jersey. She only summers in Key West. The rest of the time, she rents her house to whoever wants to live in it from September through May. Through the years we've had some interesting neighbors. A quiet cigar-chewing executive, who left the cottage cleaner than it's ever been before or since; A rowdy group of construction workers who got in a lot of trouble for trashing the place; and last year, a very young, retired, stock market whiz who spent most of his time tooling around town on one of his 13 snazzy bicycles.

Thea is understandably nervous each fall, when the search begins anew for winter tenants. She was very happy when the place was rented to service industry folks who only want to be here when the season is in full swing. She's hoping she's found some repeat customers.

"They may rent the place again next year," she says hopefully.

We like our neighbors, too. During the day, they sleep. During the evening, they work. They never take a night off. The only time we know they're next door is cool-down hour. Which is right now.

"Michael," I say, nudging him as he lies awake beside me, "where did we go wrong?"

I remind him of how simple our lives were when we were service workers, hustling tips, dragging ourselves home to spend an hour of cool-down together before collapsing, and sleeping hard in preparation for another labor-intensive day on Duval. The bills seemed smaller then, the house seemed bigger, and our cares seemed very far away.

"Life was simpler then, wasn't it?" Michael says softly.

"NO WAY!" peals the waitress next door, clear as a bell ringing in the dawn.

June Keith

Playing dress-up with my teenaged Nova Scotia nymphette nieces.
The girls found little to love at the southernmost point.

The Gift Horse Posture

In a book I bought at yoga class, the incredibly challenging postures are illustrated with photographs. First, the ideal, exactly how the pose should look. Beneath that photo, another, the reality, which is how most of us look as we attempt to execute the postures.

I thought about that book a lot last week, while my husband Michael and I hosted two nieces from Nova Scotia. It was the first time out of Canada, the first time on a plane, for both. We paid Air Canada an extra $65 to have the girls, ages 13 and 14, escorted by airline personnel through Customs at Toronto Airport, and to their connecting flight to Miami. The unaccompanied minors' parents were required to send notarized statements that the girls were traveling to Miami with their knowledge and consent, and would be met at the Miami Airport by their uncle and aunt, Michael and me.

In response to all this red tape, the girls decided it would be funny to pretend to not know us when they were at last escorted off the plane in Miami. They gazed at us blankly, then turned away. Have we changed that much since we last saw them, I wondered, as I shouted to them.

They hugged us perfunctorily and proceeded to march through the holiday crowds of the Miami Airport as if they'd done it a thousand times before. They said their ears hurt, and the food on the plane had been horrible. In Miami we ate grilled chicken at our favorite Cuban place. We bought mango shakes, to introduce them to the exotic flavors of the tropics. They were not impressed. Mango tasted exactly like pineapple they said, and that they'd tasted a thousand times before.

Because of a traffic jam in the Upper Keys, we drove most of the way home in the dark. The girls sat in the back seat, chatting and giggling and asking how long it would be before we got to Key West. We stopped in Marathon for gas and snacks at a convenience store.

"Your money sucks," they said, giggling. "It's ugly."

When we finally got home I showed them to the loft of our little conch house, and offered to make them hot chocolate with marshmallows before bed.

"Oh boy," Kaylee said, "Hot chocolate on a nice, hot night in Florida."

The last time we'd seen them, they'd been little girls. We remembered them as angels in overalls, with long hair tumbling down their backs, who loved hearing stories about the wonders of our island home in Florida, so many miles away from their tiny, rural communities in the north. Since then the girls had grown into shapely, wide-eyed beauties. We were expecting children who loved dolphins and sea shells, and the novelty of being in a summery place like Key West while the snow was flying in Nova Scotia. But those little girls were women now. As we walked with them on Duval Street, men whistled and hooted and stared.

"Hey," commented Rachel, "I've been in Key West for one day and I'm already getting whistles."

I took them to Flamingo Crossing for ice cream..

"Is this the best ice cream you've ever tasted?" I asked.

"Uh uh," Rachel said, grinning. "It's better at home."

We spent lots of time at consignment shops, since the only thing I could do to really wow them was to buy them more of the slinky tank tops and tight jeans that elicited the randy responses of their fans on Duval Street. They flew through the aquarium, museums and other attractions as if their pants were on fire. They spent an hour at the beach one day before calling home and begging to be picked up.

"We're hot and dehydrated," Kaylee said.

What they loved to do most was sit on the porch, and bask in the attention from the many men who happened by on foot, bike or car. They wrote postcards to friends in Canada. I glanced at one on the way to the post office and was disheartened to see that my niece had written, "we have to sleep in a hot, stuffy attic."

Finally, it was time to take them back to Miami Airport. The girls hunted for music suited to their tastes on the car radio while I pointed out the wonders of our 100-mile car trip over the ocean. I told them about Flagler's train, about the Hurricane of '35, about the Seven Mile Bridges, the old one and the new. Their eyes remained glued on the highway, straight ahead.

"Just look at the colors in that water," I said.

"Aunt June," Kaylee asked for the fifth time that day. "How long till we get to the plane?"

I put the gas pedal to the floor, and daydreamed about the little girls who'd charmed Michael and me for a decade of summer vacations. I tried to get into their weird, bland rock music. It sucked.

June Keith

*My great friend Sandy Arena and her mother and great friend
Teddy live in New York. They visited Key West in October, 2002,
and found it way too hot. They haven't been back.*

The Madness of Motherhood

My mother was a nurse. She worked the night shift. She left for work at 10:30 p.m. and arrived home again at 7:30 a.m. Before my little brother Rocky was old enough for school, he was often set free to roam the house unsupervised while our exhausted mother desperately tried for a few hours of much-needed sleep.

All those solitary mornings turned my brother into a very precocious kid. By the time he was three, he could cook breakfast. He made coffee for my dad. He slathered butter on Italian bread and toasted it beneath the broiler. He pushed a chair up to the stove, and scrambled eggs in a tiny frying pan purchased just for him.

One night I let Rocky help me with a school project. I was using Elmer's Glue, and Rocky became quite fascinated with the stuff. He amused himself for hours dropping glue onto construction paper, and then onto the table top and various other surfaces around the house. Then he watched patiently as the glue hardened into soft, white rubbery lumps that he scraped up and rolled between his fingers.

The next day, while I was at school, and Dad was at work and Mom was asleep, Rocky carefully poured Elmer's Glue onto her eyelids. After it hardened, Rocky shook Mom awake, to see if the glue would keep her eyes from opening. It did.

Through the years the story of Rocky gluing Mom's eyes shut has become a family classic, the mother of all stories of the amazing and terrible things my working mother endured at the hands of her free-range children.

My mother didn't have any choice in the matter of children. That's the major difference between my generation and my son's. My brothers and I were accidents, living proof of my mother's bad timing. My own son was planned, prayed and hoped for. Most of his peers were also happily invited into the world. When my mother got pregnant, she had to have a baby, ready or not. Having babies shaped her destiny. It wasn't that way for me. I got to shape my own destiny. To this day, I'm a much happier person than my own mother.

I know a woman who has twin sons. I asked her what it was like. She said it was wonderful having two new babies instead of only one at the end of a pregnancy. The next time she had a baby, a single baby, she says she felt cheated, and her arms ached with being only half full.

I know a poet with two small daughters who commemorated her own motherhood with a thick, ornate and tribalish tattoo that stretches across her beautiful belly. Wondrous. I think motherhood tattoos would become a trend if tattooing wasn't so painful. I asked her how much it had hurt.

"A lot," she answered. "But so does having babies, and that's what this tattoo is about."

I was never interested in having children, until one day, I was overcome with a powerful urge to procreate. It was beyond logic, and much bigger than any argument I could make against it. Just to cinch the deal, God sent me an utterly irresistible child. If I hadn't had my son, I would have spent my life half-crazy with missing him. I know that now.

I have a friend I call Beautiful Sandy. Her beauty, both inner, but mostly outer, has shaped her destiny. She has never married. She has never been totally swept away in love. She has never had children. Now she wants what she has missed. She is 48 years old. When I remind her that Mother Nature may have a say in whether or not she has a child at this late date, she tells me we live in an age of miracles. She has no doubt that a baby will come when she wants one. Like a push-up bra you order from the Victoria's Secret catalog.

Maybe not having babies renders you even more insane than actually having them does.

My darling friend Eileen and a pair of Fantasy Fest fairies

Jon Hynes

The Morning After

Living in Key West for all these years, I've known many Fantasy Fests and the dreaded mornings-after. I've awakened in deep purple seas of feathered boas, long, black wigs, velvet robes, fishnet stockings, harlequin hats, sequined gowns, 5-inch heels, fringed go-go boots, and all manner of glitter, satin, rhinestones, ribbons, buttons and bows. In my hot, tiny attic there is a box of stuff that tells the story of Fantasy Fest through the ages, a time capsule of Key West, told in shards and shreds of costumes, in various stages of disintegration.

There have been Fantasy Fest mornings-after when parts of my own house were unrecognizable to me, because my guests and I had dismantled lamps and wall hangings, torn apart tablecloths and bedspreads, used make-up and Elmer's Glue for unspeakable purposes in the wacky, gotta-have-a-costume frenzy that happens just before the Fantasy Fest parade.

It might surprise newcomers to the party to know that the Fantasy Fest celebration didn't always come with a handy theme the way it does now. Back in the early days of the Fest, the only thing we knew for sure was to wear a toga to Sloppy Joe's toga party.

Having found the secret to making hair stand straight up on end (egg whites, and lots of them) my friends and I used the technique when we dressed as tattooed punk rockers with spiked hair, and I'm talking way before the look was in vogue.

When my son was a baby, tiny and cherubic with blond curls and fat, rosy-cheeks, a couple of girlfriends and I decided to dress him up as Cupid, with wings and a little bow and arrow. We stapled silver tinsel all over his red flannel Winnie-the-Pooh jammies and were just about to begin applying silver eye shadow to his big baby eyelids when my Cuban husband crashed the party.

"We're turning the baby into Cupid," I said to my husband.

"Over my dead body," he said to me.

One year, I dressed that same husband in a red satin robe, with white masking-tape block letters spelling out THE UNKNOWN CHAMP on the back. Over his head he wore a paper bag, with eye holes. He wore boxing gloves, and boxing boots, and I thought his costume, based on the Unknown Comic TV character in vogue at the time, was very clever. And so did he, until we arrived at Duval Street and brutish strangers began challenging him to box.

We are no longer married.

Fantasy Fest became easier when they added the theme. By then I was waiting on tables. For "Jungle Fest" I wore a safari suit, and carried a whip. I kept my customers in line that night by snapping my whip threateningly. For the "Devil's Triangle Fest" I wore a very demure honeymoon peignoir, snow white, all lace and satin ribbons. I called myself "one of 16 vestal virgins that were leaving for the coast," a line, I think, from the song "A Whiter Shade of Pale." My gynecologist and his wife came to the restaurant for dinner that night, and were heartily amused when I told them I was masquerading as a virgin.

One year, somehow the theme was right for a diner wait-ress uniform, circa 1955, which I found in perfect condition at the Salvation Army. The dress was way too big in the waist, so I duct-taped a pillow beneath it and waited tables that night as a hugely pregnant woman. I fooled a lot of people, too. Whenever customers even hinted at giving me a hard time, I would rub my belly, arch my back, and moan a bit.

"Herb, she's pregnant, for God's sake! Don't rush her!"

I gave birth in the kitchen around ten, when I could no longer bear the burden of my terrible deception, or the agony of having my middle wrapped in 20 feet of duct tape.

These days, I go to the parade as me, just another jaded islander, flashing my breasts in exchange for beads. (Just kid-ding!!) I've seen it all before, many, many times. Nowadays, my favorite part of the morning-after is waking up long enough to turn my clock back an hour, and falling back into my pillow, for an extra hour of sleep.

Tom Netting

*The great visionary Mel Fisher, who dreamed big and won
even bigger when he and his crew finally uncovered the $400 million
Atocha treasures strewn on the ocean floor back in 1622.
For sixteen years Mel and his crew wore T-shirts that said
"Today's the Day!" while they hunted for the bounty Mel
promised was there to be found.*

A Reinvented Rose

Rose Chibbaro passed away a few weeks ago, but not before she'd chased down a couple of dreams, and had herself a very fine time in Paradise.

Twenty years or so ago, Rose found her New Jersey nest empty. Her two sons were in college. Her marriage had collapsed. Somewhere she'd read about a treasure hunter named Mel Fisher, who lived in Key West and searched daily for the lost ship *Atocha*, which had sunk in 1622 , loaded with riches. She packed up and told her family and friends she was headed for the end of the road.

"Mel Fisher, that's the man I want to see first," she said.

She did find Mel Fisher, and was soon part of the "Today's the Day" crowd of investors, divers and fans who never stopped believing they would find the treasure. Rose, a CPA, did the books.

Several years before the mother lode was found, the Fishers and friends gathered in the safe port of the Treasure Museum on Whitehead Street to wait out a threatened hurricane. Rose brought her beloved Pomeranian, Czaya.

Czaya is a Polish name, in honor of Rose's Polish roots. Czaya was champion class, but she did not mate or show because she was epileptic. The little dog was Rose's constant companion, and Rose lavished her with love and affection, just as she did all the lucky dogs she owned in her lifetime.

During the Fisher's hurricane party, several navigational charts ended up on the floor. Czaya, who is dead now, ended up on the charts, and though it wasn't newspaper, well, it was close enough, and Czaya relieved herself.

"And do you know what?" Rose liked to say, relishing the story, "Czaya pooped exactly on the spot where the Atocha was finally found!"

Rose was our accountant, and my husband Michael loved visiting her home on Bay Point. He enjoyed playing with her dogs, and hearing Rose's stories of old Key West. When Rose got cancer, she gave Michael humorous accounts of the struggle to regain her health. One day she pulled the scarf off her head to show him her newly emerging hair.

"Doesn't it look like baby bird fluff?" she asked him.

A year later, when Rose's chemo was done and her hair had grown back, Michael had cancer. Rose was there to urge him on, with compassion, laughs, and a huge stuffed animal gorilla, covered with that same wispy, baby bird fluff. She brought it to him in the hospital, just after his surgery, before his chemotherapy.

"For a while, you may look like this," she teased.

When Rose did our taxes last month, she told Michael she was feeling lousy. Then we heard that Rose's sons had taken her back to New Jersey, to live out her final days near them. The end came quickly.

Before she left Key West, while she was in the hospital here, her great friend and neighbor, Evan Rhodes, urged her to get better so that he could take her to the grand opening of *The*

Prince Of Central Park, a film based on his novel.

"Oh God," Rose said. "What will I wear?"

"That was her wonderful sense of humor," Evan says, "Because we both knew that she wasn't going to get better."

"Evan," she told him, the last time he saw her, "Czaya came to me last night. She told me she is waiting for me."

Heritage House collection

An ageless portrait of writer/artist Jeane Porter, a Key West native who grew up at 410 Caroline Street in what is now the Heritage House Museum. Jeane's famous mother entertained American luminaries like Robert Frost, Tennessee Williams, Tallulah Bankhead, Sally Rand and Ernest and Pauline (the second Mrs.) Hemingway. Jeane passed away in 2004. Her book, Conch Smiles, *is well worth a read.*

Born of the Sun

The Hemingway myth that attracts millions of tourists to his house is much bigger than the true story of Hemingway in Key West. People like imagining him as a burly macho-man, swaggering through the streets of Key West drunk and smelling of fish, a bully and a lout, who stomped women's hearts and punched the nose of anyone who got in his way. There are seeds of truth here, but those who knew Ernest Hemingway in Key West tell a far different story.

Hemingway was a man of exotic tastes. He loved Spain and all things Spanish. Key West in the 1930s was still very much a Spanish-influenced place. Imagine the delicious fragrance of suppertime black beans permeating the air he breathed as he walked up Whitehead Street to his home after an afternoon of fishing or drinking in the local color at Sloppy Joe's.

Jeane Porter remembers Pauline Hemingway's devotion to her important husband and the fine, comfortable home she kept for him. Jeane grew up in Key West, in a house a few blocks down Whitehead Street from the Hemingways. In the '30s, she was often a guest there. Jeane, a tomboy who shunned dolls and preferred running and climbing trees to tea parties, grew up playing in the spacious garden with the Hemingway boys.

"Yes," Jeane recalls, "Hemingway was a restless man. But a kind one. And a great one. This was understood by all of us."

When Jeane's father first met Hemingway, he observed: "He appears to breathe more air than most people."

Artist Mario Sanchez and his wife Rose lived in a little Conch house across the street from the Hemingways. Mario, who still lives and works on the island, remembers that Hemingway sometimes came over in the late afternoon, after a day at sea, to offer the young couple fish from the day's catch. Mario gratefully accepted the grouper and snapper, and politely turned down the sailfish.

Yes, Mario has heard the stories of the Hemingway myth, the stories of the bully and the drunk, but he can't support any of them. The Hemingway he knew was a gentleman and a good neighbor.

To set the record straight on Hemingway in Key West, as well as a number of other famous people and places from the island's history, Jeane Porter has written a memoir. In her book, *Conch Smiles*, she writes of many anecdotes involving the Hemingway kids and Pauline Hemingway.

Photographs of Pauline don't do her justice, Jeane Porter says. Pauline was very attractive, small-boned, thin and androgynous. She wore her hair short, and dressed in slacks or shorts. She was an excellent fisherwoman and hunter, taught by her famously outdoorsy husband. In Jeane Porter's written recollections, Pauline Hemingway emerges as an unsung heroine: the good, supportive woman behind the great man. Because Jeane was actually there, and remained friendly with Pauline after her divorce from Hemingway and until her death, her impressions ring sweet and true.

"Hemingway had this magical quality, this charm about him, that touched everything and everyone. He gave off light," Jeane recalls. "Yet he was no polo player; no snob. He was larger than life. We in Key West owe him a debt of gratitude. I hope we don't drown it in a flood of beer and crud and greed."

In describing Hemingway's brilliant effect on those around him, Jeane evokes a line from a poem by Stephen Spender, "I Think Continually of Those Who are Great."

"Born of the sun they traveled a short while toward the sun, and left the vivid air singed with their honour."

Joe Foote.

A very fine likeness of Key West's own Ozzie Osborne by artist Joe Foote.

Write
Whatever You Want

Stacy, a former Key West citizen, phoned the other day to question me about news of the island. I asked her if she knew Ozzie Osborne.

"Yeah," Stacy said. "What happened to him?"

"He's dead!" I said. "He shot himself in the head, on the Riviera Canal Bridge."

"Well, I'm not surprised," Stacy said. "What do you expect from a guy who bites chickens' heads off on stage?"

Of course, she was thinking of Ozzy Osbourne, the rock 'n roller. I was talking about Ozzie Osborne, the *Miami Herald* columnist, and people watcher with a penchant for irony.

I met Ozzie in 1987 when I was managing the "Richard Heyman for Mayor" campaign. Ozzie sent a check and a letter saying he was a retired journalist from Virginia, new in town, looking for something to do. I immediately enlisted him as a volunteer. As it happened, there was a job opening at the *Miami Herald*. I hooked him up with the gig. Ozzie was a great catch, for the Heyman campaign, and for the *Herald.*

He chose to retire in Key West because he loved visiting the Cayman Islands and adored the easy lifestyle of the tropics. A life-long bachelor, he bought a two-bedroom house, with lots of room for friends and family guests.

Ozzie enjoyed entertaining, and staged lots of pot-luck dinners in his early years here. He made a mean lasagna and loved the congeniality of drinking. But he couldn't hold his booze worth a damn. One glass of wine made him giddy. A second glass turned him sloppy. I don't drink, and from time to time he would question me about that, and express his fervent desire to stop. He knew he shouldn't drink, and he knew that I knew, and because of that, our friendship languished.

But oh, he could write. He wrote about priests, artists, dog groomers, chicken lovers, history, legends and lore. He wrote about barkeepers, chefs, athletes, and the dreams that propelled people to come and live in Key West. At the library, I once overheard a homeless man describing his upcoming nuptials, scheduled for the following day at Higgs Beach.

"This thing is getting big!" he said excitedly. "Ozzie Osborne from the *Miami Herald* is coming!"

A friend of mine at the *Herald* had the job, for many years, of editing Ozzie's columns. Ozzie did not enjoy having his work dissected. Once he signed off on a piece, he was done. When questioned on one point or another, he would say, in his Southern drawl, "Oh, write whatever you want." The phrase became shorthand, among my family and friends, for: "I've said all I'm going to say on that particular subject."

Elderly white males take their own lives at a rate five times the national average. Some analysts call these "rational suicides" because suicide seems to make sense when what makes life worth living is taken away, be it good health, mental capacity, or professional recognition.

There are people who believe that corporate America

killed Ozzie Osborne. Days before he died, he'd been told by *Herald* supervisors in Miami that he would have to write more columns, shoot more photos, and be in the office during traditional business hours to answer phones. Ozzie liked to work early, in the cool of the morning before things got hectic, and to finish up by noon. That's the way he'd done his job for thirteen years.

Perhaps the drinking finally got the better of him, and when every familiar thing around him began to blur, and life began to move too fast, he decided it was time to check out. Maybe he was ill. Or maybe just too weary to celebrate his 77th birthday. No one on this planet can begin to know just what Ozzie was thinking when he committed the ultimate act of despair, so, in his memory, I offer you this: Write whatever you want.

Tampa's most famous Cuban restaurant, the Columbia,
in all of its aging glory.

A Visit to Ybor City

L ast week, Michael and I spent a few days in the Tampa
area. As we were planning our trip, Mike Perez, who
lives in Gainesville, promised that he and some friends
would drive down on Friday and meet us for dinner at the
Columbia Restaurant in Ybor City. The Columbia, he said,
served the best Cuban food in the world. And Ybor City, Mike
said, was a trip.

By the time Friday night arrived, Mike Perez had canceled
our rendezvous, citing problems in logistics and timing. I was
not disappointed because I'd had enough of Tampa. It was
hot, busy and hectic, and I had no enthusiasm for Ybor City,
which, I was told, would remind me of the lower end of Duval
Street on a Saturday night. I was looking forward to a visit at
Mom's house in Sebring, a quiet town in Florida's very green
interior. But Michael had other ideas. We were going to Ybor
City and we were going to dine at the magnificent Columbia
Restaurant, with or without Mike Perez.

The only time Michael and I are not ideal companions is

when we are on the road. I like maps and plans. He prefers to navigate by the position of the sun, or the clouds, or by sheer instinct. If every car on I-75 is doing at 80 miles an hour, Michael drives that fast, too, because, he says, "you gotta keep up with the pack." If I direct him to turn off the road, he says he can't because "this guy behind me is right on my tail."

So last Friday afternoon found us flying at 80 miles an hour through the outskirts of Tampa, in search of a place called Ybor City that I think Michael imagined would rise before us on the horizon like the Magic Kingdom at Disney World. Signs eventually appeared, and soon we were cruising the main drag of Ybor City, which, just before dusk, was very quiet indeed.

We found the Columbia Restaurant, located in an ancient building that was once a cigar factory. We admired the Columbia's wrought iron gates, beautiful Spanish tiles, and cavernous, balconied rooms. The servers wore tuxedo jackets and bow ties. At the next table, I watched an elderly waiter prepare a Caesar Salad with easy elegance. Our waiter was graceful, too, deftly slipping plates and silverware out of the way as he presented the various courses of our meal.

The Columbia Restaurant did not serve the very best Cuban food I've ever tasted, but the faded Spanish motif, and the handsome waiters in their tuxedos, made it feel foreign and exotic. And I met an amazing lady in the Columbia Restaurant bathroom.

The Columbia ladies room was small and somewhat dark, with a low ceiling of drooping tiles. A woman in a white uniform, with a voice like Butterfly McQueen's in the movie *Gone With the Wind* asked me if I was having a nice time at the Columbia. I said I was. She smiled.

"Are you an attendant here?" I asked, somewhat surprised.

"I've been the lady's attendant here at the Columbia for forty years," she said proudly.

"I bet you've met some interesting ladies," I said.

She had and she named a few: "Marilyn Monroe, Rosalind Russell and Liza Minelli."

"What was Marilyn Monroe like?" I asked.

"Just like she is in the pictures," she said.

"Do you have a needle and thread and perfume?" I asked.

She did, she said, and recited a long list of other feminine needs she was capable of fulfilling. But not lipstick, she said. It wasn't hygienic. Where she kept these necessities I could not guess. The room was quite stark, and as she spoke I found myself nervously eyeing the sagging tiles above her head.

"I haven't met up with a ladies room attendant in a long, long time," I said, marveling that such a service still existed.

"Well," she said, in her high, dainty voice, "I guess you haven't dined in a fine restaurant in a long, long time."

Survivor Michael and granddaughter Leslie, atop the Key West Lighthouse, seven years after visiting chemo country.

More Than Anything

E aster Sunday, my husband Michael and I were driving down the Keys, returning home after a great family gathering in Sebring. We'd finally met our student son Mikey's new girlfriend, Natasha. Saturday night we shared a traditional Easter dinner at Mom's house. We sang and laughed and played with her little dog. Natasha told us about growing up in Korea and Germany. Our son, who is studying graphic design, showed us some of his projects.

Sunday morning Mikey and Natasha headed back to Gainesville; Michael and I to Key West. We wanted to be home in time for Michael to prepare, physically and mentally, for Monday morning and his second dose of chemotherapy.

The weekend away was a celebratory one for Michael and and me. We were celebrating having made it this far since learning that Michael had colon cancer. We'd made it through the arduous surgery, a less than glowing pathology report, and the chilling anticipation of chemotherapy. We'd made it through hours and days and weeks of reactions and reflections and prayers and meditations, and found ourselves right back where we started from: helpless and unknowing beyond the moment here and now.

In Marathon, we stopped to pick up the Sunday *Citizen*. As we drove across the Seven Mile Bridge, I read of the suicide of Key West attorney Mark Simms. I flashed on that poem you read in junior high about the rich, smart and good-looking guy, Richard Cory, who shocks everyone when he shoots himself.

I thought of Janet, my childhood friend and neighbor, a golden girl, who killed herself when we were 21. For me, the wound has never healed. I still cannot enter a church without remembering Janet's funeral, and the day of the most profound suffering I have ever witnessed, or known.

We only knew Mark Simms peripherally, the way you know of people in a small town. I learned from a friend who did know him that for much of his fine and productive life, Mark Simms had battled depression. In spite of his good looks, his many good deeds, and his loving wife and family, he'd died by his own hand. Like Richard Cory, and Janet, he'd appeared to be a person with everything to live for, destroyed by the terrible disease that robs you of the will to live.

For those who've never experienced it, depression is difficult to understand, just as you cannot truly know cancer until it comes into your life. Yet you certainly wouldn't tell a person with cancer to get over it, or to pull themselves up by the bootstraps. But that's what people with depression often hear. We respect cancer, its weird tenacity and its deadly potential. Why can't we respect depression that way, too?

I watched my husband, driving us over that amazing bridge, his beautiful hands wrapped around the wheel, his eyes intent on the horizon, his thoughts somewhere out there. I understand that Michael wants, more than anything, to live, just as I understand the moment when Mark Simms wanted, more than anything, to die.

Join us on the worldwide web at:
www.JuneKeith.com

Linda Krumel

Songwriters Chuck Krumel and Michael Keith.
Chuck offered loving support and many laughs during Michael's
time in Chemo Country. "You never know where the
next hook is coming from," Michael says.

Chemo Country

The doctors are trying to kill my husband. He's so full
of lethal chemicals he's a walking Chernobyl. It's a war,
with monthly launches of seek-and-destroy missions
designed to annihilate any renegade cancer cells that may be
lurking somewhere in his normally peaceful interior. It's like
unleashing an atomic bomb on a continent to kill 5 assassins
possibly hiding there.

We're living in chemo country.

Like most born and bred Southerners, Michael carefully
avoids discussions of his own personal physiology. He does
not like being questioned about his bodily functions or his
internal response to the warfare. So, instead of demanding
play-by-play descriptions of his roughest days and nights, I ask
him to simply sum up the battle with a line or two, which,
being a country songwriter, he does quite brilliantly.

"I slept like a baby — woke up every two hours and cried,"
he says, quoting from one of his songs.

Or, "I don't need no map to tell me where I'm at, hello

rock bottom."

Or, "It was a New York night . . . forget about it."

Last Sunday Michael summoned his early morning strength, which is often as good as it gets here in chemo country, and walked to the newspaper stand. He exited the store and spotted a man with no legs, sitting in a wheelchair.

"Can you help me out?" the man asked Michael. The man explained that the ancient wheelchair was a loaner, and that his usual wheelchair, which was motorized, had been rendered useless by the rain.

"I need a push down the street," he said.

Happy that he wasn't being asked for money, since he had none, Michael agreed. Besides, he was glad to be of service, since a country songwriter never truly feels properly utilized.

"But you'll have to hold these," Michael said, handing the man the *New York Times* and the *Barron's*.

The wheelchair was in bad shape, nearly immovable. Only one wheel turned smoothly. Michael knew the effort would cost him a day's energy, but, he thought, wasn't a man with no legs a lot worse off than a man temporarily full of chemotherapy?

He pushed, grimaced, sweated, and persevered, and the man without legs clutched the papers to his chest as if they were salvation. Finally, they arrived at the targeted corner.

The man thanked him. Michael staggered home and collapsed on the couch. After a few minutes, he told me about his adventure.

"We looked like a couple of drunken sailors weaving down Duval Street," Michael laughed. "At least we appeared to be well-read."

"And how do you feel now, Honey?" I asked him, concerned.

He quoted a song title: "Come See What's Left of Your Man."

Join us on the worldwide web at:
www.JuneKeith.com

Barlow family collection

My uncle Dick Barlow, in the winner's circle, sometime
in the 1950s. He died, very bravely, in April, 2004.

The Finish Line

Last night, late, we got a call from my Uncle Dick, a good guy who married my beautiful Aunt Phyllis when I was 4 years old. Dickie Barlow was a stock car driver, and his car was "77 Sunset Strip", named after the '50s television show. Every Saturday night back then Aunt Phyl, and as many nieces, nephews and cousins she could fit into her car, traveled to Danbury, Connecticut, to watch the handsome and daring Dickie Barlow race.

One night the 77 car was in a spectacular crash. It rolled a dozen times, skidded crazily, spewed a hail of sparks, and finally came to a jagged stop in a huge blur of dust. The crowd buzzed as ambulances screamed to the wreck site. Aunt Phyl sobbed in the middle of a circle of friends who suddenly rushed from everywhere in the stands to comfort her.

Then, in what seemed like hours but was actually only minutes, my uncle Dickie Barlow emerged from the flattened car, and triumphantly waved his arms at the roaring crowd. I never went to the stock car races again. Shortly after that,

Aunt Phyl gave birth to my cousin Alison. Saturday nights, I baby-sat, while everyone who could fit into her car, went with my Aunt Phyl to watch Dickie Barlow race.

Phyllis died of cancer eight years ago, and a couple of years after that, Dick had cancer, too. He had surgery, and people in our family said to each other, "They think they got it all," like people do. We talked about it as if cancer was a malignant egg, its deadly contents neatly encapsulated in a clearly defined marble of tumor – something to be detected and eradicated. But it isn't like that. Cancer is a sprawling monster, invisible, sneaky, covert and, most sinister of all, very fickle.

Recently Uncle Dick learned that the cancer he thought was gone with that surgery years ago, is back again, slithering its way into his glands, drilling his back with pain. He knew that my husband Michael had recently been to cancerland, had had the surgery, the months of chemotherapy, and for Christmas this year, the gift of a clean bill of health.

His voice quivering, Dick told us that he was unsure about which way to go treatment-wise. He'd been warned that chemotherapy would kill off his healthy cells. He'd been talking with a doctor in Mexico, who offered a miracle treatment and cure not yet released in America. His girlfriend had read on the Internet of a conspiracy to keep cancer alive and well in our country, because so many people depend upon the industry of caring for people with it for their livelihood.

If he took the chemotherapy, the Mexican doctor said Dick would no longer be eligible for the secret treatment and cure he offered. It would be too late. And if the chemo didn't work, Dick said, he would regret not trying the Mexican cure.

I listened to his hopes and fears, and Michael did, too. I told him I was sure there was no secret cure, and no sinister conspiracy, either. Michael did, too. Later I remembered Dickie Barlow, snaking the 77 Sunset Strip car, like a thread of liquid mercury, to the front of the pack. He won many races in those glory days. And now, he wants to win again. He wants to exit the cancerland crash site and wave his arms triumphantly at the roaring crowd of family and friends who love him. He wants to cross the finish line, unscathed.

So how do you tell a winner this: In cancerland, nobody knows until they get there, just where the finish line is?

Tom Netting

Richard officiating at Michael's and my fairytale wedding.
We're living happily ever after.

Bring Me A Higher Love

Why are lighthouses so romantic"? I once asked my husband Michael. "Because they're phallic," he answered, as he turned the page of his *New York Times*.

We have always lived in the shadow of the Key West Lighthouse. We used to have a friend who bought his house on Thomas Street because of the view of the lighthouse from the upstairs bedroom window. Later, writer Leigh Rutledge lived in the same house, and wrote in that same bedroom.

Leigh doesn't live here anymore, but he has just published a novel about his time in Key West and called it *The Cat, the Lighthouse, and the Sea* - a title that claws at the imagination.

I waited tables at the Lighthouse Cafe on Duval Street for several years before I thought to ask someone why the place was called the Lighthouse Cafe. Owner Gail Brockway wordlessly walked me around to the front of the building and pointed out, through a part in some far trees, a glorious view of the lighthouse, burning bright in the night sky.

"That's why," she said.

Shortly after I first met Michael, he told me there was something he needed to show me at the lighthouse. So we climbed the 88 steps to the very top, and as I caught my breath, he told me about how lonely he'd been when he'd first arrived in Key West.

"I came up here often in those days," he told me. "I would look at the beautiful island below and I just knew there was someone special waiting for me down there, somewhere."

Sometimes, he said, he worried that he would never meet the woman of his dreams, and that somehow, even though he was certain that she lived on the island too, a cruel fate would keep them apart. Finally, in a burst of anguish, he pulled a key out of his pocket and carved a message into the ancient paint.

"Where R U?" he wrote. Then he added his initials and the date.

He'd taken me up there to show it to me, and to tell me that he was certain that I was the lover he'd been longing for. It was wild and windy and very romantic.

I was working for Richard Heyman at the Gingerbread Square Gallery then, another place that once existed in the long shadow of the lighthouse. The next day, when I went to work, I happily told Richard of the message Michael had left at the top of the lighthouse many years earlier, and of how Michael had taken me there to show it to me, as further evidence of his love for me.

Richard smiled. Then he laughed out loud as his eyes sparkled and danced. I begged him to tell me what was so funny.

"That's a great story!" Richard said gleefully. "I bet it works every time."

Join us on the worldwide web at:
www.JuneKeith.com

Index

Order Form

Palm Island Press

411 Truman Avenue • Key West, FL 33040 USA
305-296-3102

Send _____ copies of June Keith's Key West and The Florida Keys at $18.95 each

Send _____ copies of Postcards From Paradise at $14.95 each

I understand that I may return any books for a full refund—for any reason, no questions asked.

Add $4.50 Priority Mail postage and handling for the first book and 75¢ for each additional book. For books shipped to Florida addresses, please add 7.5% sales tax per book.

Enclosed is my check for: _____

Name: _____

Address: _____

City, State, ZIP: _____

❑ This is a gift. Please send directly to:

Name: _____

Address: _____

City, State, ZIP: _____

❑ Autographed by the author

Autographed to: _____